Training on Trial

Training on Trial
*How Workplace Learning Must Reinvent
Itself to Remain Relevant*

James D. Kirkpatrick, Ph.D.
and
Wendy Kayser Kirkpatrick

AMACOM

AMERICAN MANAGEMENT ASSOCIATION

New York • Atlanta • Brussels • Chicago • Mexico City • San Francisco
Shanghai • Tokyo • Toronto • Washington, D.C.

The following marks are the property of Kirkpatrick Partners, LLC and used herein by permission: The Kirkpatrick Business Partnership ModelSM, KBPMSM, Return on ExpectationsSM, ROESM, Chain of EvidenceSM. All other marks used herein are the property of their respective owners.

Library of Congress Cataloging-in-Publication Data
  Kirkpatrick, James D.
    Training on trial : how workplace learning must reinvent itself to remain relevant / James D. Kirkpatrick and Wendy Kayser Kirkpatrick.
      p.   cm.
    Includes bibliographical references and index.
    ISBN: 978-0-8144-1464-4 (HC)
    ISBN: 978-0-8144-3814-5 (PB)
    1. Employees—Training of.   2. Employee training personnel—Training of.
  3. Organizational learning.   I. Kirkpatrick, Wendy Kayser.   II. Title.
  HF5549.5.T7K573   2010
  658.3_124—dc22   2009021988

About AMA
American Management Association (www.amanet.org) is a world leader in talent development, advancing the skills of individuals to drive business success. Our mission is to support the goals of individuals and organizations through a complete range of products and services, including classroom and virtual seminars, webcasts, webinars, podcasts, conferences, corporate and government solutions, business books and research. AMA's approach to improving performance combines experiential learning—learning through doing—with opportunities for ongoing professional growth at every step of one's career journey.

Printing number

10 9 8 7 6 5 4 3 2 1

Contents

American Management Association
www.amanet.org

Foreword by Donald L. Kirkpatrick, Ph.D.

I AM GLAD (and so will you be) that you have bought this book. It will challenge you, surprise you, and provide some very practical help as you consider the fact that you, a professional trainer, are really *on trial*.

My son Jim was visiting me a few weeks ago and took a moment to read aloud from an article he brought. The last sentence he read was, "and training managers had better consider demonstrating the value of their programs to business leaders *before the day of reckoning arrives.*" In light of current global, economic challenges, the words made perfect sense. No surprise there, as the phrase offered good advice. It was when he told me what he was reading from that I was shocked. "Dad," he said, "this is an article that appeared in the old *Journal of the American Society of Training Directors*. It was written by you in November 1959!"

We discussed the fact that fifty years ago I understood that it was urgent for learning and performance professionals (we called them "training professionals" back then) to be able to create and demonstrate value to the business. Today, that could not be truer. Many of you have not realized the implications of having a jury looking at and making judgments about your impact, your value, your budget, and subsequently, your future. And if they haven't challenged you yet, the "day of reckoning will come"—perhaps sooner than you can imagine. And you had better be ready to defend yourself when you plead "not guilty" of having a budget higher than you can equate in terms of benefits versus costs.

The first thing to do in preparing your case is to learn my four levels for evaluating your courses, programs, and learning function. In case you aren't familiar with them, let me share them with you (see also Table F-1).

- Once a learning event of any kind has been delivered, Level 1 comes into play. I call it *reaction*. I define this as a "customer service" assessment of how participants reacted to the program. This includes querying such matters as the delivery of the program, the materials, the facility, and the perceived usefulness of the content.

- Level 2 is *learning*. Many times it is important to know to what degree participants increased their knowledge, skills, or attitudes, based on their participation in the program—or at least to determine if they left with a satisfactory acquisition of the intended KSAs (knowledge, skills, attitudes).

- Next comes Level 3—*behavior*—which answers the following questions: "To what degree did participants apply what they learned on the job? If not, why not?" It seems to me that learning is generally a waste of time if people don't use what they learn.

- Finally, Level 4 is *results*. This tells us to what degree the targeted outcomes actually occurred as a result of the learning event(s).

So, I challenge you to first understand the "science" of this book—the concepts, theory, principles, and techniques that Jim and Wendy have provided. Then, I challenge you to perfect your "art" by studying the details in the book and selecting the applications that fit your own situation.

That way, you can be sure that your judge and jury will agree that you are "not guilty."

TABLE F-1. The Kirkpatrick Four Levels

Level 1: **Reaction**	To what degree participants react favorably to the learning event.
Level 2: **Learning**	To what degree participants acquire the intended knowledge, skills, and attitudes based on their participation in the learning event.
Level 3: **Behavior**	To what degree participants apply what they learned during training when they are back on the job.
Level 4: **Results**	To what degree targeted outcomes occur, as a result of the learning event(s) and subsequent reinforcement.

Preface and
Acknowledgments

WE SURVIVE and thrive when we understand that our role as workplace learning professionals is not to deliver training programs but *to extend learning* from episodic interventions to continual on-the-job enrichment. Ultimately, our role is to deliver demonstrated value to our business partners. This book provides a template for creating, delivering, and measuring the value of your training efforts within your organization or for your clients. Along the way we provide examples from companies and professionals who have used the model and achieved results.

Here are a few general comments about the book. It is not a textbook or a training manual. Instead, it is more of a storybook, with the expanded metaphor of a courtroom and real-life examples and anecdotes. The reasons for this are threefold. First, there are already many textbooks, articles, and manuals outlining techniques for being an effective business partner, yet many still have not found the way to make this *happen*. Second, we personally think you will *learn and be inspired* more through sto-

American Management Association
www.amanet.org

ries, metaphors, and best-practice examples than you will through models, diagrams, bullet points, and a lot of supportive narrative. Finally, we think and train in terms of metaphors because *people relate to and remember them.* Also, the words *training* and *learning* are meaningful to different people in different ways. Therefore, we decided to use either or both at different times. But basically, we mean what goes on at Levels 1 and 2.

Training on Trial includes several features that will allow for easy understanding and application. Boxes and highlights set these elements apart from the descriptive narrative and include helpful tips, practices to avoid, best practices from successful organizations, and some of our own experiences. But the key to understanding the concepts in this book is the metaphor of a United States civil courtroom trial. This completes the training—individuals, departments, and the entire training industry—in their work of delivering true business value.

We hope this book inspires you to look at your role as a workplace learning professional with a fresh new perspective. And that a new perspective leads to increased business results.

Acknowledgments

We would like to offer heartfelt thanks to the following people for invaluable contributions not only to this book but also to the field they proudly represent. First of all, our stars—Mike Woodard, Heidi King, Nick DeNardo, Bindu Gangadharan, Annette Charlton, Jim Hashman, Rebecca Knapp, Fiona Betiviou, Deana Gill, Sheila Barnett, Linda Hainlen, and Joy Serne. Other key contributors were Don Murphy, Corinne Miller,

Sandy Almeida, Paul Gregory, Diederick Stoel, Tom Trifaux, Major Abdulla Abood, and our very special Brunei window washer, Chai. Finally, our deep thanks go to Don Kirkpatrick: father/father-in-law, guide, and inspiration.

Training on Trial

1

The Case Against Us

"We are confronted with insurmountable opportunities."
—Pogo

ON THE MORNING OF November 14, 2003, I was summoned
to the office of the new CEO, Robert Warrington, of First Indiana Bank, where I was serving as the Director of Learning and
Development. Since he took over earlier that year, Robert and I
had had several informal conversations about training, the Indianapolis Colts, local restaurants, and world travels. Our interac-
tions were cordial, friendly, and productive. My job had been an
enjoyable and worldwide experience for eight years.

I made sure I was all decked out that morning—even wore a
suit and tie. I was not sure what was on Robert's agenda, other
than it was "training related." I arrived at my office early
enough to brush up on the latest initiatives my L&D team of six
members was in the midst of, and I thought up a few new ones

in case Robert was interested in expanding our influence to the thousand or so bank employees.

I rode the elevator up to the twenty-eighth floor, where I was summoned into Robert's office right on time. As I walked through the door, something happened that had never occurred during my prior visits. I heard a "click" as the large wooden door shut behind me. I began to wonder what type of meeting this was going to be, as I walked the twenty or so steps to Robert's expansive, polished mahogany desk, where he sat with a rather somber look on his face. My next thoughts came quickly, one on top of the other. "Uh, oh . . . something is wrong— trouble of some kind, just like being called to the principal's office. He is going to give me bad news."

After exchanging some nervous pleasantries, he got right to it. "Jim, we have decided to make a change in the way we do training here. I have decided to eliminate the positions of the six trainers on your team. I want you to stay, however. I have confidence in you that you can carry on alone, and can utilize the fine business managers we have to pick up the slack."

In recent years, this scene has recurred many times for many people. It takes different forms, but the message is remarkably consistent: Executives have become wary of the value that training brings to the business in relation to the investment that is made. Research by several major training-related groups clearly shows that learning professionals and training departments that emphasize the *training event* as key to business results are particularly vulnerable to this type of action.

I learned a valuable lesson that day back in 2003. *My department had been on trial and we didn't even know it!* And worse, the verdict from the new CEO was, for the most part, "guilty." I vowed back then to no longer count on good relationships between "us trainers" and our business partners—or the great programs we deliver. Instead, I concentrate now on understanding what our stakeholders—our key business partners—*expect from us*. I focus our training, reinforcement, and coaching efforts not only on creating strategic value but also on demonstrating that value. I also vowed to help as many people as possible to prepare for the time when they may find themselves on trial.

In 1959, ASTD published Don Kirkpatrick's articles on the four levels. In the first article, Kirkpatrick cited Daniel Goodacre's work with BF Goodrich and quoted Goodacre: "Training directors might be well advised to take the initiative and evaluate their programs *before the day of reckoning arrives.*" Many still need to heed that warning from over 50 years ago. The tradition that training value comes mostly from design, development, and delivery (Levels 1 and 2; see Table F-1) is imbedded in the world's learning culture. This book is designed to offer—nay, shout—yet another wake-up call: Learning professionals at all levels and in all types of organizations *must extend their roles beyond tradition*. To help you achieve this end, we've provided a model and the specific steps that will help you become a genuine strategic business partner. Additionally, we've scattered many "business partnership tips" throughout the book, and these are applicable to professionals in any situation. For example, here's the first such tip.

> **Business Partnership Tip:** Take an honest and objective look at your job, role, and function as if you were a practicing attorney. What evidence can you provide to demonstrate your value to the bottom line of the business in relation to your efforts?

Introducing Our Metaphor

Let us begin by introducing the metaphor used throughout this book: the civil trial. In civil cases, an action is started when a *plaintiff* files a *complaint.* The *defendant* then receives a *summons.* These terms, in this context, are defined in the vocabulary of the training community:

- *Complaint:* This document states what the *defendant* has done that supports the notion that the cost of learning efforts has exceeded the benefits those efforts have brought to the business.

- *Plaintiff:* This is the party who brings an action; in the training context, it is the business stakeholder who complains in a professional action.

- *Defendant:* This is the party against whom the improvement is sought, or the learning professional.

- *Summons:* This is any indication that there are questions or concerns that the training or learning is not bringing about satisfactory bottom-line results.

Most of you will not receive a summons slid under your door, informing you that you are being accused of producing learning efforts that have not provided enough value to the business. However, it *is* likely that there have been conversations going on, either with you or around you, discussing the value of learning in relation to its cost. It is also likely that at some point you will be "brought in for questioning." And it doesn't matter whether you are working in a large company, in a small training group, or as an independent consultant. The charges are being brought against *all of us,* whether we are workplace learning professionals, training departments, organizational development groups, professional associations, or major elements of human resources—in short, the entire learning community.

Unfortunately, until we receive official notice that we are being looked at with a critical eye, we think it applies to others. For instance, associations and corporate universities may think that they are immune from prosecution; individuals may assume that they are safe within their organizations, groups, and powerful associations. The bad news is that we are all subject to likely prosecution. The good news is that, for most of us, there is time to do something about it.

In the past three weeks, we have had a number of friends and colleagues ask us to look at their résumés because they have just been laid off. About half of them were surprised to be back in the job market. We have also heard of three training departments that were slashed to bits—anywhere from 30 to 100 percent. And others are sitting on pins and needles, waiting while the jury on their work is out for deliberation and the "verdict" is forthcoming.

There are a lot of data and much information on, and lobbying for, the fact that learning investments are as strong as ever, that business leaders are asking for the muscle to meet demanding needs that will arise in the future. We are not buying that argument, however. We think business executives are asking for increased profits, increased customer retention, decreased costs, and reduced risks. They are *not* specifically asking for a reduction in the skills gap or an increase in employee engagement. We also think they are aware that they are losing many top performers, but they are not necessarily making the connection that trainers can do much about that situation.

Trainers face a corporate jury that *may or may not* formally convene to decide the value of their contribution to the organization versus the expense of their operations. By *corporate* we include all organizations, including public sector and not-for-profits. This corporate jury is not necessarily the same as the one who charged the trainers in the first place, but most often it is. There are also instances where a single individual sits in judgment; in that case, trainers have a judge, not a jury, but the *judgment* is the same. These are the decision makers—in this case, making decisions about your future. So, let's add another definition to our judicial lexicon:

> ▸ *Jury:* The body of persons, or person, selected from the organization or client base to hear evidence and decide the relative value of your training program.

Continuing the Metaphor

Now, here's another tip.

> **Business Partnership Tip:** Ask senior business leaders in your organization how they think training is bringing value to their functions.

What evidence might your judge and jury have against you already? Information that is working against our case comes in two basic forms: research and anecdotal.

> ▸ *Evidence:* All relevant manner of evaluation data and information that is presented to the judge or jury, in order to persuade them to come to certain conclusions.

Research Evidence

There is, unfortunately, a lot of research that suggests that training and consulting, in and of themselves, do *not* lead to positive business outcomes. For example:

1. A University of Phoenix study in 2004 showed that 26 percent of learning effectiveness occurs *prior* to a learning event, and a full 50 percent of learning effectiveness comes as *follow up to* the learning event (Peterson, 2004). Incidentally, the same study found that 85 percent of training investment dollars were put into the 24 percent of what is left over—the learning event itself (see Figures 1-1 and 1-2).

2. An ASTD (2006) study identified the causes of "training failure" (i.e., training's failing to lead to expected results). It found that 20 percent was caused by events and circumstances *prior* to training. Ten percent was caused by sub-par delivery of the programs. And 70 percent was due to problems with what they called the "application environment." The latter consisted primarily of two factors: participants not having the opportunity to use what they learned, and

FIGURE 1-1.   Activities Contributing to Learning Effectiveness

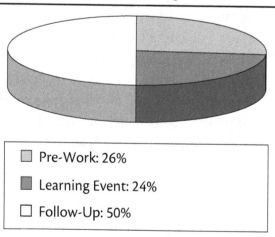

☐ Pre-Work: 26%

■ Learning Event: 24%

☐ Follow-Up: 50%

FIGURE 1-2.   Typical Learning Investment

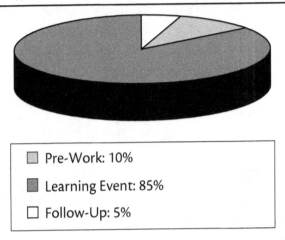

☐ Pre-Work: 10%

■ Learning Event: 85%

☐ Follow-Up: 5%

nonreinforcing supervisors' actions following training (see Figure 1-3).

3. Rob Brinkerhoff (2008) described a study that queried a large number of employees who had recently gone through training about the application of what they had learned. Fifteen percent reported that they did not try the new skills; 70 percent said they had tried and failed; and only 15 percent were able to achieve sustained new behaviors (see Figure 1-4).

4. A Josh Bersin (2008) study showed a strong trend toward informal learning. Twenty percent of job-relevant learning was found to occur *prior* to formal training programs, 10 percent during training, and as much as 70 percent as on-the-job learning (see Figure 1-5).

Findings such as these seem to refute what we, as learning professionals, have held sacred for decades: that the design, devel-

FIGURE 1-3.   Causes of "Training Failure"

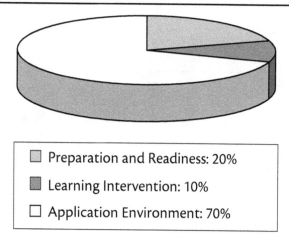

☐ Preparation and Readiness: 20%

■ Learning Intervention: 10%

☐ Application Environment: 70%

FIGURE 1-4.   Training Application

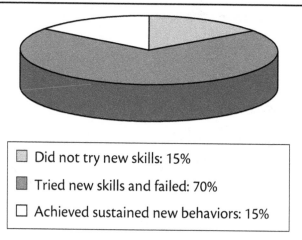

☐ Did not try new skills: 15%

■ Tried new skills and failed: 70%

☐ Achieved sustained new behaviors: 15%

opment, and delivery of training programs provide value to an organization (see Figure 1-5).

FIGURE 1-5.   Where Learning Takes Place

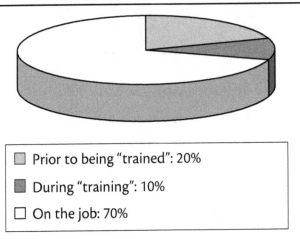

☐ Prior to being "trained": 20%

■ During "training": 10%

☐ On the job: 70%

Business Partnership Tip: Do your own research as to what are reasonable expectations or outcomes, based on your training budget. Consider the program using half the budget or double the budget, and do the same exercise.

Anecdotal Evidence

Executives in organizations get information from all kinds of sources, including conversations around the veritable water cooler. They hear comments about consultants, trainers, learning events, and possible causes of goals not being met. Most of these comments seem to be negative. Oftentimes, business leaders are under the gun to increase revenue and earnings per share, decrease costs, and improve customer relations. In government and not-for-profit agencies, the categories and targets may differ, but the pressure is the same.

When times are good, the comments focus on who is responsible for the success. Following is an account from a colleague of ours with a large Minneapolis company:

> *My training colleague and I were invited to sit in the back of the room while the Senior Vice President of Sales went over the positive quarterly numbers with a room full of sales leaders. [Note: they didn't have a seat at the "table," but at least were in the room.] The SVP was going out of his way to congratulate everyone in the room (especially himself) for the fine work, but never did he mention the role that training provided. Near the end of the meeting, my colleague leaned over to me and said, "Some of that is ours!"*

This, of course, is not what we want to have happen. Evidence is surely heaped on all of the "true" producers—the sales force. This situation is not exactly good testimony for the value of training. The problem here was that, while the two learning professionals *intuitively knew* that their team had made a great contribution to the bottom line, they had no hard or soft evidence to show it.

One of the major traps trainers have set for themselves is to reinforce the notion that training by itself leads to positive bottom-line results. For example, consider the hospital network on the West Coast that in 2003 received a corporate directive to improve its patient-satisfaction scores. The Learning and Development Department immediately switched into high gear to achieve this end. Targeted training was designed, developed, and delivered to every employee in the hospital, under a program called "Our Service to You." Unfortunately, at the end of the year, the patient-satisfaction scores had not improved. They tried again in 2004—again, with minimal results. And again in 2005, 2006, and 2007. Each time they changed the name of the program, and changed some of the activities, but basically it was the same program each year.

Here is the rub. The Learning and Development professionals *knew* that participants had learned the intended knowledge and skills. They were competent when they left the classroom or switched off their computers, but *something happened after that* that caused the failure. They suspected that there was a lack of support and accountability from the managers to reinforce what had been learned, and therefore new skills were never transferred to sustainable, targeted behaviors. The truly unfortunate thing is that they had no *evidence* to suggest that the problem was not in the material or the training but in the follow-up. Therefore, the trainers had little choice than to follow the annual insistence from business leaders to "run the training again."

We wonder how many more chances those trainers will get before "the day of reckoning arrives."

Training Alone Is Not the Answer

The question trainers must ask themselves is: Are we guilty? Much of our training and consulting work during the last few years has had to do with first *creating* value and (only) then *demonstrating* that value. We are afraid that, in a lot of instances, the training industry is indeed guilty of not bringing relative value to the business. On average, we spend little time and few resources preparing the participants (and their supervisors) prior to training, so as to maximize their learning during the training.

We spend even less time reinforcing what the participants have learned so that the knowledge and skills will transfer to sustainable, on-the-job behaviors. Thus, we are guilty of not providing nearly as much value to the business as we could.

> **Business Partnership Tip:** Carefully consider new training requests in terms of an overall business plan. What value to the business is the training intended to provide, and what pre- and post-training support are possible?

We are also guilty in another sense. When we do provide value to our internal and external customers, we don't always do a good job of *demonstrating* that value. Wendy and Jim are frequently called upon to conduct impact studies for our clients. So, we ask our clients to identify two mission-critical programs or processes that we then evaluate in terms of ultimate value to the business, name the success factors in doing so, and make recommendations to improve and leverage the impact going forward. Many of the professionals with whom we work are quite capable of conducting and administering the same data review, holding the interviews, meeting with the focus groups, and conducting the surveys that we do, but either they don't have the time or do not have enough credibility with their business partners for their results to be believed.

Four-level *evaluation* is designed to improve all types of programs (both formal and informal, and the processes) leverage learning through Level 3, and ultimately facilitate the development of a *Chain of Evidence*^SM to demonstrate the value of the training.

A good friend and colleague of ours at a major Midwest U.S. manufacturer recently said to us: "Please caution your readers about something. Just because senior leaders are not *asking* for you to provide evidence that your worth exceeds your expenses, don't be fooled into thinking that you are on solid ground. I have seen instances where these executives *report* a strong belief in training, development, 'our people are our strongest asset,' and so on. But when budget time comes and there are cuts to be made, they almost always start with training."

We could not agree with that statement more! When Jim worked at First Indiana Bank as a training director, the boss was good about telling him what was expected of his department and him. Unfortunately, her expectations were typically described in terms of pleasing the internal customers more than in achieving favorable business results. We were able to meet those expectations for almost eight years. By the time Jim received his "summons" from Robert, the new CEO, it was too late to gather and present the evidence that would have found a decision in our favor. Instead, Robert went around to many of the bank's neighborhood branches and gathered his own evidence. So the verdict for Jim's team came back as "guilty"—not enough of the right kind of evidence to convince the executive to keep his whole team.

Have You Already Been Summoned?

Perhaps you have already been summoned, but don't realize it. Or maybe it's coming any day now. Here is how you can begin to prepare for your nearly inevitable summons—or determine if perhaps you have already received that summons and didn't recognize it:

1. *Don't wait for a summons to begin action.* Don't wait for the judge or jury to convene to review the evidence at hand and make a determination about your future. Instead, be proactive. Put together your own plan, gather your own evidence, build

your own case, and ask for an audience with a judge or jury *before they ask you.*

2. *Be vigilant for cues that you have been summoned.* Here are some typical signs that you have been given a summons:

- A business partner or other senior executive asks you to show them ROI (return on investment)—in this case, *your* return on investment!

- You hear, "You certainly run a lot of programs and always seem to be busy, but we are considering putting more emphasis on revenue-generating activities."

- "Would you please send us some suggestions for budget cuts?"

- "We are thinking about hiring someone to do an impact study on our onboarding process."

- "Does anybody know why we keep losing our best people?"

- "Renegade" training groups or related initiatives are springing up, apart from your training department. You get the feeling that they are doing so to avoid you or your team.

- As an independent consultant, you are told by a client, "We are going to wait on that."

- "We are wondering if we can make better use of our managers as trainers. What do you think?"

It is wise for you to respond to these charges or inferences in some way. If you have been diligent about being a true business partner and have gathered evidence to demonstrate your value to the business, then you might even welcome the challenge to prove your worth. Now begins the process of doing so.

Wendy's Story

It was the late 1990s and I was a product manager for a consumer goods company in the Midwest. It was a high-pressure job, where new products needed to be developed and brought to market quickly. Being the product manager, I was also the project manager and at the helm of what I could best describe as organized chaos.

We had a new product for the largest home improvement center chain, and the timeline was no different from that for any other product: "How fast can you have it in stores?" Daily, I simultaneously created, updated, and completed tasks on the Gantt chart. Each day was a drill in how fast I could get things produced and delivered.

One day near the launch date it was time to work on the training materials for the new product. This is where I need to come clean with you, and tell you that we in marketing laughed at our training manager; we found her a bit silly, certainly not a "trusted business partner." Rather, she was an obstacle to overcome or, better yet, to avoid altogether. She seemed to have no bearing on reality when it came to delivery timelines or what might be reasonable to accomplish. So in most cases, I created some "training" materials on my own and left her out of the mix.

This product was really important. It required a multistep measuring and cutting operation to be performed in the store by the hourly associates, so it really needed some good training. Mistakes meant more scrap and more returns, which would be costly and cut into our profits. Profit margins were already thin, so anything we could do to preserve them was important. The professionally designed training materials really weren't optional.

I met with the training manager to start the formal training request. The meeting went as I had come to expect: I explained the project and the timeline; she responded with what I thought was an unrealistic, ridiculously long amount of time to produce the required result; I left feeling frustrated; she was most likely thinking that I was not very pleasant to work with. Then, one of those unexpected things happened. (These unexpected things always seemed to occur close to a launch date, so I'm not certain why we even call them unexpected anymore—we could just call them "predictable.") The training manager had a terrible accident. She sustained a head injury and her return to work was unknown. She was the only training professional in the company, so I was on my own to create training materials for the new product.

So, I did what any good product manager would do: I created some training materials as quickly as possible. I traveled to a store location to do a combination train-the-trainer with a national sales manager and a training session with a team of store associates. Then I returned to my office and started working on the next product launch. I didn't really give that training another thought.

Key Points

- There is strong evidence from multiple sources that training events alone do not yield significant business results.

- All training and learning professionals are being watched and judged to see if their value to the business exceeds their expenses.

- Even if you are not being asked to show the value of your training, you need to gather the evidence of your value and proactively present it to your jury.

American Management Association
www.amanet.org

References

American Society for Training and Development (ASTD) (2006). *State of the Industry Report 2006*. Alexandria, VA: ASTD Publishing.

Bersin, Josh. (2008). AMA Blended Learning Webcast, October 1.

Brinkerhoff, Robert O. (2008). "Training Impact Evaluation That Senior Leaders Believe and Use: The Success Case Method." Workshop presented at Training 2008 Exposition and Conference, Atlanta, GA, February 4.

Goodacre III, Daniel M. (1957). "The Experimental Evaluation of Management Training: Principles and Practice." B.F. Goodrich Company, *Personnel*, 34 (May).

Kirkpatrick, Donald L. (1959). "Techniques for Evaluating Training Programs." *Journal of the American Society of Training Directors*.

Peterson, Brent. (2004). Unpublished paper from Apollo Consulting Group. University of Phoenix.

2

Taking the Case

"Don't think there are no crocodiles because the water is calm."
—MALAYAN PROVERB

YOU ARE STILL READING, so we trust that you have encountered something that has convinced you that it is in your best interest to demonstrate the value of the training you provide. Remember, particularly in times of economic uncertainty, businesses must carefully evaluate *all* of their expenditures, including those for training.

The good news is that if you learn and apply the principles in this book, you will have a much better chance of winning your case for training. As a bonus to you and your company, you will expand your influence in that business, enabling it (and you) to thrive like never before. We believe that most business leaders—your corporate juries—want to find in your favor, but they will do so only when you bring significant value to their bottom line, which you can demonstrate in terms they understand.

There is even more to be gained. You have the opportunity to make a difference—and be given proper recognition for your contribution. Business leaders the world over are looking for competitive advantages—like no other time in history. Margins are tight; competition is strong; the markets are up and down like a yo-yo. *Now is your chance to show that training can provide a significant competitive edge.* Case in point: A consultant from Booz Allen Hamilton was telling us that his team streamlined an instructor-led training program from five days to three days by eliminating redundant content and by adding two e-learning modules. This was accomplished without compromising the integrity of the content, the learning, or its ultimate impact. That is the kind of edge many executives are looking for. And one of the keys to the program's being so well received was that the changes were made *before* anyone asked for them!

So there has never been a greater opportunity for trainers to create both an individual and a collective legacy in the world in which we work. Likewise, there has never been a greater sense of urgency to do so, in part because there is one legal term that trainers do not have the luxury of claiming:

> ▸ *Insanity plea:* A claim by a learning professional that he or she lacked the mental capacity at the time of delivering training that had no measurable value and that he or she should not be held responsible for it.

So let's get started. The secret to making a believable justification for training is to become a *strategic business partner*. Take a look at the photo on page 21. It illustrates both a challenge and an opportunity.

The rock formation on the left side, with all its lush foliage, represents "the business." The formation on the right, with its sparse vegetation, is the world of learning and development. The thin rocky structure between them is the bridge that connects the two worlds. Note also the narrow span and the swirling waters below it.

While on vacation in Aruba, we were driving along and saw a sign that said NATURAL BRIDGE 7 MILES, with an arrow pointing to the right. Hey, who doesn't want to see a good natural bridge once in a while? So we turned right and drove down the road in anticipation of soon finding this treasure of nature. To our dismay, when we got there all we saw were the remains of where the natural bridge had been. For this natural wonder, the day of

reckoning had arrived. Don't let your training programs fall victim to the same fate.

> **Business Partnership Tip:** Try to attend strategic planning sessions with the business's executives. They can help you recognize how to best leverage your training. It is also important to know firsthand what your strategic directives are so that you can best focus your efforts and allocate your budget.

Evaluation and the Four Levels

We refer to much of what we see in training evaluation today as *checkmark training*. What we mean by this is the overreliance on reporting indicator metrics, such as the number of courses in a catalog, the number of attendees, the training hours in an employee's file, and so on. Well, checkmark training is not cutting it anymore. Belief that your contributions to an organization offer stand-alone worthiness, and that you have a "get out of jail free" card because of those efforts, is fast disappearing. The trainer's efforts, programs, and processes are not the end; they are the means to the end. And the end that business requires trainers to accomplish is that of having a positive impact on business results, in whatever form that those results might take.

> ▶ *Checkmark training:* Measuring the value of training based on consumptive metrics, including the number of courses available and the number of hours of training completed.

There is a word that many trainers embrace, and they believe it is their flag in the ground: *learning*. We hear and read that word so much, and in so many contexts, yet it has become like fingernails on a chalkboard for us. That's because the word *learning* represents the dock where we have missed the boat, and it is one of the reasons training is on trial.

Look at the four levels shown in Table 2-1: reaction, learning, behavior, and results. Learning is solidly sitting in Level 2 (it *is* Level 2), and historically, this is what happens for the participants in the classroom. Trainers develop and teach to *learning objectives.* Many of the titles of articles in the training journals have the word *learning* in them. We are members of a *learning team*, and many of us are in *Learning and Development* departments. In summary, what we are doing as trainers is to reinforce the belief that we are about delivering programs—and that job is done when the participants walk out of the classroom.

Combating the propensity of learning professionals to stop their efforts at Level 2 is our purpose in writing this book. We feel there is a need to clarify the original intent of the Four Levels, which were created by Don Kirkpatrick in the 1950s. That is, while the four levels are widely known, few trainers are using them to their full potential.

TABLE 2-1. The Kirkpatrick Four Levels

Level 4: Results	To what degree targeted outcomes occur, as a result of the learning event(s) and subsequent reinforcement.
Level 3: Behavior	To what degree participants apply what they learned during training when they are back on the job.
Level 2: Learning	To what degree participants acquire the intended knowledge, skills, and attitudes based on their participation in the learning event.
Level 1: Reaction	To what degree participants react favorably to the learning event.

On page 26 of *Evaluating Training Programs: The Four Levels* (1993), Don Kirkpatrick wrote:

> Trainers must begin with desired results and then determine what behavior is needed to accomplish them. Then trainers must determine the attitudes, knowledge, and skills that are necessary to bring about the desired behavior(s). The final challenge is to present the training program in a way that enables the participants not only to learn what they need to know but also to react favorably to the program.

While these words have characterized our and Don's writings, we have not provided a detailed process for using the four levels; indeed, we take some of the blame for incomplete use of the

FIGURE 2-1.   The Kirkpatrick Business Partnership Model[SM]

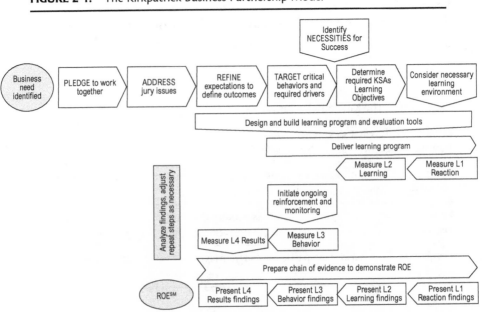

model to this point. Here, in this book, we unveil the new Kirkpatrick Business Partnership Model^SM (KBPM)^SM, which fills this need for a process and provides the guidance to leverage the full power of the Kirkpatrick Model.

Introducing the Kirkpatrick Business Partnership Model^SM

The KBPM is a simple model—the concepts behind it are easy to understand and the steps are clear. However, if workplace learning professionals were already doing what the Kirkpatrick Model suggests, this book would not be necessary! So we urge you to hang a copy of the natural bridge photo on your wall while you internalize and practice the steps in the KBPM. This will lead you to a new level of importance, relevance, and value to your company.

We have talked about the KBPM for several years in our training programs. The idea initially came from the work of Jim and Dana Robinson, pioneers in the field of performance consulting. One of our biggest challenges in developing the model was to produce a detailed model that would work in multiple functions—for individual practitioners, teams, and entire learning functions.

Over the past few years, we have used these fundamental concepts with individuals and teams around the world. We fine-tuned them at organizations with thousands of employees and others with only 100 employees. We have also applied the model's precepts to work with private corporations, not-for-profits, and government agencies. So we proudly introduce our newest model, validated by the examples and case studies described in this book.

As there are seven steps to the KBPM, these steps are individually explained in Chapters 4 through 10. Additionally,

Chapter 3 offers the foundation and basic principles for the model and introduces our star contributors. But before we begin, here are a couple additional tips.

> **Business Partnership Tip:** Provide your business partners with a copy of the KBPM. That way, you can discuss the training program with them, building a chain of evidence that supports your contribution to the bottom line.

> **Business Partner Tip:** Rewrite the job descriptions of all learning professionals in your organization so that their duties, influence, and impact extend beyond Level 2 (Learning) to Levels 3 and 4 (Behavior and Results).

Wendy's Story

We left off the story in Chapter 1, with the new product launch and the execution of my training program. About six months passed, and I was reviewing purchases from the retailer, as I do weekly when they were reported. They weren't what we expected. This product was one in a series of similar products. It should have been a slam-dunk. So what was the problem?

I conducted some analysis. I reviewed the product rollout. The only thing that seemed to be different about this product's introduction was the fact that I had created and conducted the training myself. Could it actually be possible that the *training* was the cause of the poor sales? At that time I did not have the tools or expertise to determine if this really was the case, but it seemed like the most plausible explanation. While I had done what I knew at the time, my training program was basically a lecture on how to size the product for the customer. Yet sizing the product accurately is a multistep process that I know now would have lent itself to hands-on training, with a knowledge demonstration at the end. Sales reps reported that the aisle where the product was housed was the most feared and avoided in the store. Associates didn't really understand how to cut the product, so they stayed away from it in the hope that customers wouldn't ask them to do it.

The product was eventually discontinued, resulting in a very expensive buy-back of unsold units. It was a hard lesson. The silver lining for me, however, was the realization that perhaps training *does* matter in bottom-line results. That day I vowed to understand training better.

Fast-forward to 2001. I had a new job, with a different consumer-products manufacturer, also as a product manager. The product was wire closet shelving that could be cut to size in the store aisle by an associate. The situation was similar to my past job, in terms of the pressure to develop products and get them to market. This time, however, there was no training professional on staff. Product managers were expected to develop their own training materials and conduct train-the-trainer sessions. And the results were similar. Sometimes the store associates understood how to measure and cut the product, sometimes they didn't. Similar to the other product I had managed, the store associates ran from the aisle so they wouldn't need to display their ignorance to customers. Sales suffered as a result.

Sales in general were not great at this time. Then, the September 11, 2001, tragedy occurred at the World Trade Center and pretty much everything ground to a halt. Sales dropped, travel was canceled, and the United States collectively recovered, but quietly. By February 2002, enough time had passed that I, and everyone else on my marketing team, thought our jobs were safe.

I was setting up for a line review with the second largest home-improvement center in the United States. I was dirty and sweaty. I had cuts on my hands from trying to move the heavy pallet racking myself, and from quickly assembling one of each of our products with limited tools. It was 2:30 in the afternoon and my cellphone rang. It was my boss's boss, calling to tell me that our division was being closed and we would all lose our jobs in three months or less.

I stood in disbelief. Then I cried. I called my mom and cried some more. The marketing team was working so hard, and sales were up slightly, despite the poor year. How could we all be losing our jobs? Well, I didn't have long to dwell on it. The line review was the next day. Executives were flying in that evening, and they wanted to see the completed set around 10 PM. So I did what anyone in my position would do: I had the finest lobster dinner to be had in a small town in the Carolinas. I had a few glasses of cheap wine. I got the crying out of my system. And I continued setting up for the line review until 3 AM.

The next morning came all too early. The line review went great. No one would have known that all of the people presenting it were soon to be unemployed. Yet I had no idea at the time that getting laid off from that job was actually a lucky event, a turning point in my career. With the layoff from that company I received outplacement counseling. A quiet woman named Marilyn was assigned to help me figure out where I would go next. I went to my appointment with her with one idea: pretend I know nothing about myself. Do all of the tests and analyses. Read the results, and let them tell *me* what I should do next. She agreed and I began taking tests. The next week Marilyn and I met to review my test results. She told me what they said, and what they indicated I should do next. The results were shocking to me. And life-changing.

Key Points

- Training professionals have an unprecedented opportunity to make a huge impact on their organizations by becoming strategic business partners.

- Research tells that we need to redefine our roles as learning professionals by extending our influence beyond the development and delivery of training programs and into the business itself.

- The KBPM is a systematic way to create and demon-strate training's value to an organization.

Reference

Kirkpatrick, D. L. (1993). *Evaluating Training Programs: The Four Levels*. San Francisco: Berrett-Koehler.

3

The Foundation
of Our Defense

"Use what talents you possess, for the woods would be a very silent place if no birds sang there except those birds that sang best."
—HENRY VAN DYKE, U.S. AUTHOR, EDUCATOR, AND CLERGYMAN

REMEMBER OUR metaphor of the trial? Let's take it a bit further. The best way to defend yourself is to first create value for the business and then to demonstrate it to your corporate juries. Ultimately, what you need to do is facilitate the following changes: Convert yourself into a *strategic business partner* and help convert your business partners into *strategic learning partners.*

What does this mean? You need to take another look at that photo we introduced in Chapter 2—the natural bridge.

Notice the first italicized term above: *strategic business partner.* You have to decide that your role as a training professional

needs to be expanded to involve ways that you can influence employee performance and ultimately have an organizational impact. This means crossing over from that bare rock to the lush, green side of the natural bridge.

Next, notice the second italicized term: *strategic learning partner*. Here's how we define that term.

- *Strategic Business Partner:* A learning professional who recognizes that his or her worth is evaluated by the business impact or outcome of the work he or she supports.

- *Strategic Learning Partner:* A business professional who recognizes the role that learning professionals play in the accomplishment of key business outcomes.

Crossing Over to the Other Side

We were recently presenting the "natural bridge" metaphor to a group of St. Louis professionals. One insightful woman, Melinda, commented, "You know, most learning professionals would prefer to take the bridge across. At first glance, I saw it as the only way. But I have tried that route in my company and have been turned away. I tried to make a business case for working together, but the senior managers basically told us to 'Go back to where we belong.' Do you know what I am going to have to do? I am going to have to climb down from the right side—our side—to the water, swim across, and then climb up the other side. It will take longer, and is also fraught with danger, but it is my only chance."

Taking the "high road" requires walking across the bridge and being received on the other side by your partners in business. It may mean the executives allow you to be part of the teams that include strategic planning and execution; it may mean meeting with department heads to determine how you can help them achieve their goals; it may mean eliciting the help of supervisors with Level 3 evaluations. Oftentimes, it requires having an executive at the top—a CEO or key board member—who *gets it*. Or, rather, who gets what learning professionals do—that training is an investment, not merely a cost. It implies that there is some *willingness* on the part of your business partners to engage you and give you a chance to prove your worth.

Melinda was apparently having trouble achieving that engagement. As many of we trainers find, our efforts to come across the bridge are met with, "Go back to where you belong [i.e., designing, developing, delivering, and spending *our* hard-earned money]." Melinda likely does not have an executive "champion" or even some willing business leaders to help her cross over. But rather than be discouraged, Melinda is going to find another way. She's going to use the grassroots approach or, in this case, the climb-and-swim method.

The business leaders in Melinda's company may truly believe that her job is to deliver training programs and make sure that people show up. The business managers' jobs, on the other hand, are to "run their business" while ensuring that training participants get their "checkmarks" for the training hours.

Take another look at the photo of the natural bridge. The climb-and-swim approach has three components, as Melinda described it: The first is to climb down the right side (or the learning side), and this means becoming an expert on the business side, learning the language, operations, structure, and identifying the key players. It means preparing your materials—the evidence for your defense—and sealing it in a waterproof container. In learning terms, this involves selecting one or two key programs, preparing for and implementing them with a full business partnership approach, and carefully gathering the data to prepare your case for the jury on the other side. If you do not as yet know what that entails, you will by the end of this book.

The second component is the swim across. Once you have your case ready, you enter the water and begin to swim across the divide. All bridges aren't across troubled waters, but yours may be—the water may be frigid, maybe even turbulent. You'll have to navigate your way through the "watery" world of business, and in this case it means taking the "low road" because the jury has *not* requested that you present your case. To the contrary, you will have to use your influence to secure that opportunity to present it. Do you know what is hard about that? Getting their attention and securing their time to hear your case. They are the jury because they make the budget decisions, but they don't know that you have a case to present. (Remember, you are presenting your argument, not defending yourself!)

Once you reach the base of the left side, you are ready for component three: the climb. Melinda will not be able to make that climb to the top in one effort, nor will she be able to convene her jury immediately when she reaches the top. More likely, she will have to settle for presenting her case to a lower court jury, perhaps even a lower court judge. In the world of the learning professional, that may mean a couple of mid-level managers, a senior vice president, or a group of sales managers. Whatever the situation, the initial or grassroots presentation must be sound in order to get you the chance to reach the true decision makers.

> **Business Partnership Tip:** Suggest a gathering of your organization's leadership and training teams, and use the natural-bridge photo to lead a discussion on how well your business and learning functions are working together.

Note: We recommend crossing that bridge if you can. But if the way is blocked, be assured that there is another means to becoming a strategic business partner. We discuss that later on. But, our purpose in this chapter is to provide an overview of the seven steps in the Kirkpatrick Business Partnership Model.

The Seven Steps

Here is a brief overview of the steps in the Kirkpatrick Business Partnership Model (KBPM).

Kirkpatrick Business Partnership Steps						
P	**A**	**R**	**T**	**N**	**E**	**R**
Pledge	**Address**	**Refine**	**Target**	**Necessities**	**Execute**	**ROE**
to work together	important jury issues	expectations to define outcomes	critical behaviors and required drivers	for success	the initiative	Return on Expectations^{SM}

Step 1: Pledge to Work Together

The KBPM (see Figure 3-1) starts with *someone* initiating a request for help with a business problem. Unfortunately, this request rarely comes in a clear message like, "We need to increase our sales in the southwest region about 15 percent in the next six months. Do you (Training and Development) think you can help us with that?" Or, "We want to increase by 25 percent our retention of those we have identified as high-potential employees. Are there any training programs that can help us to accomplish that?"

Instead, you are more likely to hear, "We need new sales training. Do you have anything?" Or, "Please develop a leadership program for our mid-level managers." Worse, of course, is if they don't ask anything of you at all.

Pledging to work together actually begins *before* the request for help. It starts with building a relationship of listening to and understanding the overall needs and direction of the business, and your earning some trust from those executives in charge in

FIGURE 3-1.   The Kirkpatrick Business Partnership Model

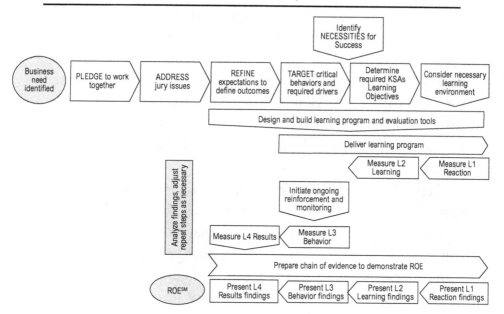

order to elicit the actual request. This pre-step may require you to make an effort to find out, any way you can, what the biggest needs, problems, and business opportunities are in your organization. It also involves your understanding and embracing the role of learning professional as a means to support the key initiatives of the business to increase benefits (revenue, profits, market share) or to diminish its liabilities (accidents, lawsuits, scrap). So, in fact, there is no such thing as a "training initiative." Instead, your role is to conduct training and reinforcement that supports a business initiative.

When you are convinced that this is the role you want to play, talk with your business leaders to make sure they agree that a cross-functional team will meet their business needs—and that they want you to be on that team.

Step 2: Address Important Jury Issues

There are three issues regarding your case that you need to address. First, you need to identify who is on your jury. It doesn't matter if you work for a large corporation, a government agency, a small family business, or are an independent contractor—you have a jury. While that jury changes depending on the particular initiative at hand, there is an individual or a group of individuals sitting in judgment of you and your impact on the business.

Second, you have to ask that jury what its members expect your initiative to deliver. This entails more than merely asking, of course. The initial expectations that you hear expressed will likely need to be stated in terms that you are comfortable with—whose results you can deliver through your training and reinforcement efforts—and that the jury feels will satisfy the business need.

Third, you need to research (or just ask) what type and format of evidence will be viewed as credible. For example, your CFO probably wants to see different evidence than will your marketing manager.

Step 3: Refine Expectations to Define Outcomes

With the jury expectations clarified, the next step is to convert these expectations into targeted, observable, measurable Level 4 outcomes. This is a component of the process that many professionals believe they do, but few actually accomplish.

Let's consider the natural bridge metaphor once again. When a training program has been selected and the expectations are determined, it is no easy task to convert these elements into tangible outcomes. That is, don't expect to just stroll across the bridge, meet your business partners, and expect them to accept your plans straight away. Chapter 6 (Step 3 in the process) offers a series of questions that will help you facilitate the conversation with your jury so you can solicit from them the measurable outcomes they are seeking.

A colleague, Corinne Miller, was formerly an engineering business leader for Motorola before she became dean of their Corporate University. She once said, "When I was with the business side of Motorola and someone from Motorola University would show up with a blank tablet and ask me, 'What are your expectations for our program?' I would send the person away with the response, 'Part of that is *your* job: to tell me what I should be able to expect from you!'" The lesson here is that you need to have your consulting hat on when you cross the bridge and meet your jury. You need ideas that will give you some realistic outcomes for the training program—outcomes you believe you can deliver and that will still satisfy the expectations of your business partners.

Remember: *The end is the beginning.* All your efforts should be focused on the outcomes your jury wants you to achieve. These outcomes usually necessitate specified training, coaching, support, accountability, and incentives, as well as anything else you might offer in your program. If your efforts don't support the desired outcomes, you don't make a strong case for your contribution to the business strategy!

Many people ask us, "What's the difference between expectations and targeted outcomes?" Well, expectations are typically expressed in top-of-the-mind, first impulse, and generic goals; in contrast, targeted outcomes are indicators of success that are observable and measurable. Typically, it takes a lot of discussion to identify the measurable indicators you will need for a training program. For example, management may express an expectation of greater safety on the job. The corresponding targeted outcome would be a reduction in the number of lost-time injuries on the job.

> **Business Partnership Tip:** Articulate the goals for your training group in terms of the jury's expectations and targeted outcomes.

Step 4: Target Critical Behaviors and Required Drivers

Once the targeted outcomes are identified, you can gather input on to how those targets will be met. You will work with your jury members, or perhaps the key managers and supervisors, to identify two key factors: *critical behaviors* and *required drivers*. This step is often overlooked, but don't you fall into that pit. This step is your key opportunity to shine, so perform it well.

Critical behaviors and required drivers are key to reaching a successful Level 3, and ultimately to successfully meeting your targeted outcomes. So, this step is critical to your business partnership and your strategic learning efforts. Let's examine the definitions of these terms.

- *Critical behaviors*: The few key behaviors that employees will have to consistently perform in order to bring about the targeted outcomes.

- *Required drivers*: Processes and systems that reinforce actions, monitor procedures, and encourage or reward performance of critical behaviors on the job.

Critical behaviors have to be *consistently performed*; otherwise, your training efforts will not bring about the targeted outcomes.

Required drivers are the processes and systems incorporated after the training that encourage the desired new behaviors, monitor their execution, and reward their successful adoption on the job. These drivers most commonly are performed by support and management staff, and include coaching and feedback, and, ultimately, holding employees accountable for applying newly acquired skills to the job. For example, drivers might include observation of work, quarterly awards for adherence to procedures, and training graduates monitoring their own progress.

Do you understand the difference between behaviors and drivers? The required drivers support the training and provide accountability for the key behaviors that employees need to apply on the job to bring about the targeted outcomes. When selected well, these tools act as *drivers of performance success*. For this reason, drivers are every bit as important as the critical behaviors in predicting the successful outcome of a training initiative. Indeed, the importance of monitoring both critical behaviors and required drivers cannot be overstated. This monitoring acts as an early warning detection system; when you know what is causing substandard performance, you can intervene to remedy the problem.

Step 5: Necessities for Success

One of the key elements in the Kirkpatrick model is that it does not isolate the impact of training events. The business partnership is integral to the KBPM, as is the gathering of evidence for and demonstrating the value of delivering and leveraging training efforts. It is a collective effort.

With that said, there are variables that can negatively affect the targeted outcomes established in the earlier steps of this process. You, therefore, want to mitigate as many of these variables as possible. We mentioned required drivers as important *after-training* events. Now, we need to consider what occurs *prior* to training—the prerequisites, or *necessities for success*, that help set the required good conditions for that success and head off the problems before they occur or become too large.

> ▸ *Necessities for success*: Prerequisite items, events, or conditions that set the stage for success and help avoid problems before they reduce the impact of the training initiative.

Examples of such necessities for success are preparing or laying the groundwork for a culture of coaching that will leverage and reinforce newly learned skills, setting up software programs to streamline the new processes, and clarifying the reporting and accountability structures. Required drivers are ongoing support processes and systems, necessities for success are more often events or projects. These events and projects likely involve communications to the organization describing the initiative and training mentors and coaches to reinforce the training.

Step 6: Execute the Initiative

You will notice that there is no single step in the KBPM diagrams called "Execute the Initiative." This is because this sixth step contains multiple components. If you are familiar with the ADDIE model of instructional design (Analyze, Design, Develop, Implement, Evaluate), this step encompasses the D, D, and I. In terms of the KBPM, this step includes the following:

- Determine the required KSAs (knowledge, skills, attitudes) or learning objectives
- Consider the necessary learning environment
- Design and build the learning program and evaluation tools
- Deliver the learning program
- Measure Level 1 (Reaction)
- Measure Level 2 (Learning)
- Initiate ongoing reinforcement and monitoring
- Measure Level 3 (Behavior)
- Measure Level 4 (Results)
- Analyze findings, and repeat or adjust steps as necessary

There are two major differences between the ADDIE model and the sixth step of the KBPM. First, the evaluation tools are established at the same time as the learning program is, thereby ensuring that they are fully integrated and will measure elements of value. Second, the bulk of time during this step is focused on reinforcement and monitoring after the training—issues that the ADDIE model does not really address.

The good news is that, whereas you are probably spending a lot of time right now developing learning materials and delivering training programs, you will spend less time with the KBPM. By this point in the process, you have already clearly defined the behaviors that will bring about the desired business outcomes. All you need to do is design and build your training program to teach those behaviors.

Where you will be spending your time, however, is in supporting the critical behaviors and their required drivers. And at the same time, you will be *managing the expectations* of your business partners by providing regular status reports. These reports will show how the on-the-job behaviors and drivers are changing, and will hint at the preliminary impact of this training on the desired business outcomes.

Do you have control over all of the systems and processes? No, but it is your job as a strategic business partner to make it as easy as possible for your business partners—your supervisors, human resources, and IT staff and managers—to uphold their end of the partnership by collecting and providing data on a regular basis.

Step 7: ROE^SM (Return on Expectations^SM)

This step is of utmost importance, yet it is rarely performed in the real world. *Return on Expectations* means taking the data collected at each of the four Kirkpatrick levels, putting it into a logical Chain of Evidence, and presenting it to your jury in a compelling manner. In the model, this step involves the following components:

- Present the Level 1 findings

- Present the Level 2 findings

- Present the Level 3 findings

- Present the Level 4 findings

If you want your business leaders to regard you as a true business partner, you have to excel in this final task. This step may sound like a brief and simple add-on, but it is not. For mission-critical initiatives, it can make or break the verdict on your activities, which can greatly impact your future as a learning professional, as well as the future of your department.

Your jury members are probably required to collect this type of data for all of their initiatives, as well as provide it for their own projects. Without backup data, they would not receive their budgets. So part of becoming a valued business partner is walking in their shoes, gathering data and presenting it professionally, in the way with which they are familiar. This is critical to gaining their respect and trust.

Case Studies and Best Practices

Making a business case for the power of the KBPM is going to take more than just say, "Take our word for it." So, let us introduce our top ten ambassadors for this process—those individuals who have taken all or part of the model and put it into practice in their organizations. These programs were used in both the United States and Canada, and their details are presented in this and subsequent chapters (see Table 3-1).

Note: We purposely included three leadership programs because so many people ask us how soft skills can be measured with hard data. We also chose as an example the implementation of a software process, as we were told it "couldn't be done" using the Kirkpatrick Model. By the way, as with the companies identified in Jim Collins's book *Good to Great*, these are *our* stars. Since our model is quite new, not all of our stars began their initiatives with our model in mind.

(*Text continues on page 48*)

TABLE 3-1.   Eleven Superstar Examples Using the KBPM

Organization	Superstars	Showcase Program	Focus of the Evidence
Georgia-Pacific Consumer Products Manufacturers and distributors of towel, tissue, and tabletop products for the retail channels	Mike Woodard, Director, Georgia-Pacific University	Managing remote team members, and entire approach to learning and development at Georgia-Pacific University	Entire model, with emphasis on front-end alignment and back-end leverage of business managers; includes cross-functional advisory board
Department of Defense, Military Health System Patient Safety Program	Heidi King, Deputy Director, Patient Safety	TeamSTEPPS, a training and implementation initiative focused on using teamwork principles for safer healthcare deliveries	Entire model, along with team training and change management theorists, with emphasis on the front end; includes data-driven program improvements and facilitation of executive involvement
Edward Jones Financial services company	Strategic Learning Services Department	Financial Advisor Training Program	Entire model for learning programs involving thousands, and an approach to internal consulting
Comcast Cable Provider of cable television and wireless service	Jim Hashman, Director of Sales and Retention L&D	New sales training program	Entire model, focusing on a compelling chain of evidence

Region of Waterloo, Ontario, Canada. Municipal Government	Organizational Development	Learning to lead leadership program for non-supervisors	Entire model, with emphasis on pre-positioning of training, action planning, and action learning; includes plan for dual account-ability and coaching guide
AEGON Canada Inc. Financial services company	Fiona Betiviou, Manager, Training and Development	The Leading Edge, a leadership program	Using Level 3 data to repurpose 12-module leadership program; includes monitoring, reporting, and making recommendations
Ministry for Children and Family Department, Vancouver Island, Canada Provincial government child welfare agency	Deana Gill, Senior Manager, National Learning and Development, Pricewaterhouse Coopers	Action Leadership Program	Monitor drivers and indicators of success; leveraging the entire model to develop a positive culture of engagement and personal leadership responsibility
Allen County Department of Transportation	Melanie Barnes, Training Specialist	Road Sealing Process	Entire model from an individual contributor's perspective; targeted training and extending one's role and value into the business

(continues)

TABLE 3-1. (Continued)

Organization	Superstars	Showcase Program	Focus of the Evidence
Clarian Health Indianapolis-based health-care organization	Linda Hainlen, Manager, Informatics Education	Medication charting and scanning software implementation program, stabiliz-ing glucose process	Focus beyond "the (implementation) event" to include defining success, pre-positioning, targeted re-inforcement, and reporting
Farm Credit Canada Financial service company for Canadian agriculture	Joy Serne, Director, Culture, Learning & Employee Experience	Overall corporate culture change	Making a business case for change, setting up a system of mutual accountability, and measuring/reinforcing results

Wendy's Story

When we left off in Chapter 2, Marilyn, my outplacement counselor, had analyzed my personality inventories and was about to tell me "what I should do with the rest of my life."

"Wendy," she said, "It is clear to me that you are good at a lot of different things. However, that doesn't mean that you enjoy all of these things or should do them." She continued, "I see in your career history that you were offered a lot of different opportunities, and it seems you took them all, whether you would like them or not. There is nothing wrong with this; I am sure you learned a lot along the way. Now, however, what I would like to see you do is carefully consider what you *want* to do. What you are passionate about. Where you think you can make your mark, and at the same time be happy in your work."

"I see what you mean," I said. "I have never had the opportunity to choose my work. I always just took the 'best' job that came along. I never really allowed myself the time to think about it."

"Right," Marilyn said.

"Okay," I said. "I have a sense of the things I like and don't like, but what do the tests say I would be best at?"

"The tests," Marilyn said, "indicate to me that you would be an excellent corporate training professional."

Dumbfounded would not begin to describe how I felt that day. I looked out the window of the 14th floor outplacement office at the rooftops and trees. I am seldom at a loss for words, but that day I was. Training? That silly, unprofessional, disrespected, HR-ish area? I thought some more. I did have to admit that when we had seminars conducted by outside professionals I often found myself thinking, "I wish I had *that* job." Many people had told me over the years that I was good at public speaking. And I really didn't mind it, either. And I had certainly seen the results of poor training. Maybe Marilyn had something here.

"Okay," I said. "I'm game. If I wanted to consider a position as a training manager, how would I get there from here? My education is in retailing. My career experience is in marketing. I have done some training, but I am not sure I would call it 'good.' What do I need to do if I want to basically change professions?"

Here is where my good luck, as it turned out, continued. I had made some contacts with another consumer-products manufac-turer a few years prior. I had stayed in touch with them. When I let them know that I had been laid off, one of them called me back right away. Jeff—someone who had become a friend as well—said, "Wendy, you won't believe this. We have just created two new posi-tions and I think you would be great for them." He continued, "They are regionally based, so you could stay in St. Louis. The job is a hybrid. Half of it is marketing, and half is training. You would have to travel a lot, but I think you would be perfect."

The ironic thing about all of this is that I had never told Jeff that my outplacement counselor had suggested that I look into corporate training positions. And out of nowhere comes a job where my marketing experience would get me in the door, and I would have the opportunity to learn training! After a series of interviews, I took the job. Quite lucky, don't you agree?

Key Points

- There are two ways to cross over from the training side to the business side: walk across (by executive invitation) or swim and climb (grassroots approach).

- Studying the steps in the KBPM will help you create and demonstrate your value to the organization.

- There are professionals who act as trailblazers as they implement these training principles.

4

Step 1: Pledge to Work Together

"It's amazing what you can accomplish if you don't care who gets the credit."

—HARRY S. TRUMAN

THE KIRKPATRICK BUSINESS PARTNERSHIP MODEL (KBPM) begins with the deliberate decision to enter into a partnership with business leaders that is designed to impact their bottom line. This step does not mean simply getting the word from a senior executive that he or she wants you to deliver a training program on sales skills, and your purchasing or designing a training intervention to meet that request and delivering on it. Indeed, all too often this is how business and training interact. Business says, "We want a training program," and training says, "Okay," and so it goes. But it doesn't have to be that way.

To begin, let's take a look at the first step in the process: pledge to work together.

Kirkpatrick Business Partnership Steps						
P	**A**	**R**	**T**	**N**	**E**	**R**
PLEDGE	Address	Refine	Target	Necessities	Execute	ROE

The Pledge

To illustrate the right way to begin Step 1, let's get right into our stars—our examples. Michael Woodard, good friend and colleague, is the Director of the Georgia-Pacific University. In other words, he is their Chief Learning Officer. Mike has earned the proverbial "seat at the business partnership table" through his current exceptional work at Georgia-Pacific Consumer Products and his prior work as the Director of Sales Training at PepsiCo. See what Mike does when he gets a request for a training program.

Georgia-Pacific Consumer Products Best Practice #1

"When I get a request for sales training from one of my business partners, I first get together with them to determine what brings them to ask. For instance, is there a problem with sales numbers, or a new opportunity with a new market segment, or a new product, or is there some sort of corporate directive that will require a substantial increase in sales? Once I am clear about that, we have a discussion as to whether training will make a significant contribution to the need. We carefully look at other options, identifying all that will likely be required to bring about the desired results. If we decide training is indicated, we spend time determining my business partner's—or, in Jim's term, my jury's—expectations. Typically we have to do some negotiation here to ensure that not only will training (and subsequent reinforcement) be able to create the desired impact but also that the expectations will be satisfying to our business partners.

"Another way we built a case for partnering with the business was through the development of an Advisory Board. This is a group of leaders from Georgia-Pacific Consumer Products—with representation both from the university and from the business. The business leaders are directors and vice presidents to ensure that we build strong alliances."

Figure 4-1 is an example of an agenda from a recent meeting:

Figure 4-1.   Example of an Agenda from a Recent Meeting

Meeting Purpose: A 2008 Update and Look Ahead
Date of Meeting: Monday, June 16th, 2008

Desired Outcome	How (Process)	Who	Time
1. An update on the Sales University staff, so everybody is aware of the capabilities moving into the second half of '08 and into '09.	Discussion	Mike W	15 min.
2. Your feedback on the Training Needs Assessment re-cap binder, so that we can make any adjustments for the 2008 assessment.	Discussion	Group	15 min.
3. Review the 2008 workshops completed to date and the Level 1 evaluation scores, so that we are all aligned around this low-level evaluation feedback.	Update & Discussion	Mike W	0 min.
4. An understanding of our Level 2 assessment (Testing) strategy and timeline, so that we are all aligned and set up for success.	Understanding & Confirmation	Group	30 min.

5. An understanding of the New Hire Orientation program and release, and how to best prepare hiring managers and yourselves to leverage this powerful tool to its fullest potential.	Update	Group	30 min.
6. An understanding of what Score Carding metrics some corporate universities are using, so that we can formulate our university Score Card with total alignment.	Discussion	Group	45 min.
7. A review of the MVI e-Learning curriculum and your feedback, so that we can share that feedback with MVI.	Discussion	Group	15 min.
8. An understanding of how "pilot" workshops are conducted, so that we are all aligned on expectations and format.	Understanding & Discussion	Group	15 min.
9. A review of the team training scheduled for the remainder of this year, so that we are all aligned around the topics and dates.	Discussion	Group	20 min.
10. Review of universities policies and several attendance issues, so that we are all aligned around each policy and its reason for being.	Review & Discuss	Mike W & Group	15 min.
11. An understanding of each of your 2009 and beyond priorities to the best of your abilities, so that we can continue to align to your needs.	Discussion	Group	30 min.
12. Feedback for the university, so that we can better serve your needs for the remaining part of 2008 and into 2009.	Discussion	Group	15 min.
13. An agreement on next steps, so that we are all set up for success moving into 2008.	Review	Mike W	10 min.
14. Plus/Delta of the meeting.	Discussion	Mike W	5 min.

We will hear more from Mike and the Georgia-Pacific Consumer Products example in later chapters. Meanwhile, our colleagues at Clarian Health, in Indianapolis, also find the concept of a cross-functional advisory team (they call it a Learning Council) helpful in generating support for the business partnership model. Linda Hainlen, Manager of Informatics Education, provides us with some insights as to how they are doing just that.

Clarian Health Best Practice #1

"In our journey to provide excellent learning to our users, we, as many others, were concentrating almost solely on the 'event.' Oh, we had done some creative 'before event' advertising and even some prerequisite e-learning. However, we never really concentrated on the 'after the event' learning. We met the requirements—we had excellent attendance, received wonderful comments on our smile sheets, and obtained very high scores on our classroom assessments! We thought we were doing a great job. By most standards, we were. However, we had been ignoring the 'after the event' learning that really gains performance, not just knowledge.

"We have found that it has been helpful to convene a Learning Council on a quarterly basis to drive this business partnership model that Jim introduced to us. [The Council] is primarily made up of educators throughout the organization, but we are attracting business people to our meetings to create a stronger partnership and more synergy."

We have met with Clarian's Learning Council and found them to be extremely open to the new ideas of the KBPM. Many went back to their individual training and business units to spread the word about possibilities for leveraging learning with the help of key business partners.

> **Business Partnership Tip:** Do what you can to initiate the development of some type of learning council, made up of a combination of learning and business leaders.

At Clarian Health, they also made the Learning Council fun! It is important to do whatever you can to make your business partners *want* to join forces with you. As an example of this, the photo below is the invitation the Learning Council developed for one of their meetings:

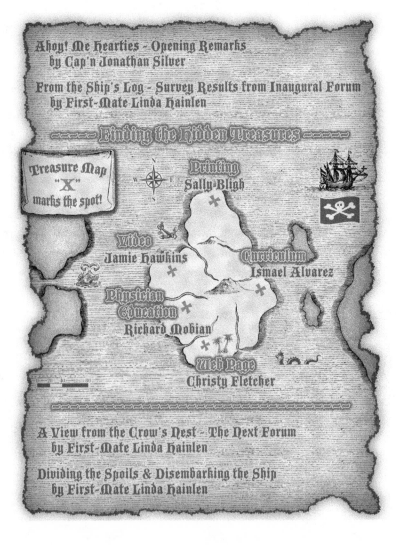

Support from the Top

Jim has done work with L'Oreal in Paris and elsewhere in France. During one of his visits, prior to working with the training leaders, he was invited to spend some time with the business executives. Do you know how they started the meeting? "Jim, please tell us how we can support training." That really helped set the table for the great success that L'Oreal has experienced.

Others have had the great fortune for there to be leaders at the top who "get it." These CEOs realize that training and follow-up are the keys to achieving their business directives and goals. Farm Credit Canada is one of those organizations. Farm Credit was started in 1959, and today it is Canada's leading provider of agricultural financing and business solutions. Jim spent some time talking with Joy Serne in Regina, Saskatchewan, recently. To be honest, it was her *title* that so intrigued him: Director of Culture, Learning, and Employee Experience. Here is what he leaned from Joy about the unique company.

Farm Credit Canada Best Practice #1

John Ryan, CEO, saw the importance of aligning training with the business when he took over in 1997. He realized that employee engagement scores and business results were lower than he liked, and those translated into a less-than-satisfactory customer experience.

While the company was full of talent and good intentions, something was "getting in the way" of maximum success. There was a low-trust environment where employees were fearful of making mistakes; short-term results were not leading to sustainability; results were more important than the people who created them.

John Ryan decided to create a "culture where people feel inspired to come to work and to give their all for their colleagues and customers." He knew that in order to do this, he had to use training and the business, along with strong leadership, to create a culture of 100 percent accountability. This meant that internal leaders and workers would have to become committed partners.

A series of communication and training events, followed by targeted reinforcement and performance management, were launched in 2003 to support the transformation of the FCC culture. This business partnership eventually led to sustainable increases in employee engagement scores along with a doubling of the business portfolio.

Sure, many companies and CEOs *announce* that they intend to create a culture of accountability, but few know how to put that into practice, as Farm Credit Canada did. The book *Say It Right the First Time*, by L. Malandro (McGraw-Hill, 2003), outlines the steps they took.

Another organization from Canada, the Region of Waterloo, Ontario, has also had the great fortune of getting some top-down support for their business partnership model. Rebecca Knapp, an OD Consultant for the Region of Waterloo, offered the following helpful insights into how they leveraged this.

Region of Waterloo, Ontario, Canada, Best Practice #1

At the Region of Waterloo, the *Corporate Vision and Values*, as well as the closely aligned *Seven Core Leadership Characteristics*, is the springboard for the blending and working together of training with the business. Senior leaders champion the cross-functional effort, and business leaders look expectantly to their training counterparts to help them achieve their commongoals. Together, they have developed a *Learning Opportunities Calendar* from which they plan their training in accordance with the needs of the city (the business). The Organizational Consultants, like Rebecca Knapp, are a strong go-between for training and the business.

An example that Rebecca shared with us was the opening of a new museum in the existing Doon Heritage Crossroads. As staff size grows dramatically and people learn new jobs, existing skill sets are measured against the Region's *Seven Core Leadership Characteristics* to determine where support and development is required. Appropriate coaching and training is then provided along with standard new employee/new manager training programs to ensure individuals possess the behaviors and characteristics necessary to flourish in their new roles.

Forming a Partnership from a Mandate

Our colleagues at the U.S. Department of Defense (DoD) knew how to get off to a good start, in part based on a U.S. congressional mandate. In 1999, the Institute of Medicine (IOM) released a landmark report, *To Err is Human: Building a Safer Health System*, which led to a national outcry and forever changed the face of medicine in America. In the report, the IOM estimated that preventable medical errors in U.S. hospitals cost an estimated 98,000 lives and $17 to $29 billion every year. The IOM further concluded that medical errors could be dramatically reduced by making fundamental changes in our national health-care system—changes that embrace the reality of human fallibility and that build safety nets to prevent human errors from leading to patient harm. A key IOM recommendation was that health-care organizations "establish interdisciplinary team training programs for providers that incorporate proven methods of team training." In 2001, Congress released a mandate that the DoD integrate medical team training into all its health-care operations.

Even before the release of *To Err is Human*, and the mandate, the DoD Patient Safety Program recognized the urgent need for medical team training, and began to build the TeamSTEPPS™ program. Before even scoping the initiative, they spent time advocating and building the training/business team that would be responsible for addressing this critical need. Full details of their work to date can be found in Chapter 11.

> **Business Partnership Tip:** When you are making presentations about the value of training, make sure they include data that will be meaningful to your audience.

Grassroots Approaches

Let's look at another organization and see how they are in the midst of building a chain of evidence to proactively take before the jury—a jury that the trainers requested convened to review their case. This best practice comes to us from colleagues at the Department of Transportation for a large county in the Midwest. For sake of discussion here, we refer to it as Allen County Department of Transportation (A-DOT).

Professionals in the Human Resources Training and Development Department (HRTDD) at A-DOT included Melanie Barnes, the Senior Employee Development Specialist. This best practice has been used successfully by a number of organizations over the past two years. The term *impact study* is not a new one, but the way it is used here, specifically with the Kirkpatrick four levels, makes it an extremely powerful presentation to gain the commitment of executives to the business partnership model. Here is how A-DOT is implementing the plan, according to Melanie.

Allen County Department of
Transportation Best Practice #1

As Melanie explained, Jim came and worked with them recently, highlighting and showcasing two programs the department had developed and delivered. One was for roller equipment operations, which had to do with repaving roads, and the other was a "softer-skills" program about organizing and prioritizing the workday.

Jim conducted impact studies on those programs, including what the department had done right, what it could be doing better, and how to present his and the department's findings to leaders in other departments. For the next year, the HRTDD decided to conduct its own impact study for a program on the road-sealing process, another type of road repair. First, HRTDD developed a plan for selecting just the right program to take to the "jury." They made sure the program solidly aligned with corporate strategy and that they had business leaders behind them so that the results would be successful in the eyes of the stakeholders [aka the jury].

They then developed the training, set the table for success among the participants, and reinforced the training through Level 3 evaluation and follow-up. Now, their plan was to put it all together in a compelling "chain of evidence" in order to have a positive impact on the jury members, who were the county stakeholders, who ultimately were responsible to the taxpayers.

They believed that, by going through this process, they would convince the business units and other training departments at the agency of the power of the Kirkpatrick Business Partnership Model, implemented in the A-DOT way. This would increase the respect they get from other business units in the government and would allow them more opportunities to bring value to the county.

The A-DOT's human resources department got it. They were using a program—done in the best way they knew how, complete with relevant data at each of the four levels and delivered to the jury with style and power—to make it easier to get invited across that bridge the next time, and the time after that.

> **Business Partnership Tip:** If you can't follow the standard channels to integrate your training initiatives into the key business strategy, consider a grassroots approach.

Be Careful What You Ask For

Jim received a phone call from a well-known European cosmetics company a couple of years ago, and the training executive said, "Jim, we believe we are a successful training department, but we do not get much credit for it." Jim asked him how he knew, and he said, "While we deliver a lot of programs and get good attendance, they [the business] rarely contact us to help them with their business challenges."

Well, we decided to conduct an impact study and present it to the senior business leaders. We heard that the presentation (to the jury) went well, and we then didn't hear anything for a while. After about six months, we received another call: "Jim, we need your help again." We were dumbfounded.

"I thought you guys really did a terrific job of demonstrating your value!"

"Apparently we did," he said. "We now need your help in prioritizing the requests we get from the business."

So: fair warning. If you do a good job with this step of the process, you will likely be asked to come across that bridge on a regular basis—and *be expected to make a strong contribution on that same regular basis.*

The Region of Waterloo and Clarian Health both used data to build strong cases for the business partnership approach. Specifically, Waterloo used employee-satisfaction data to awaken the leaders of the municipality to the importance of developing a program for nonsupervising leaders. And Clarian used both patient and employee feedback to implement a partnership approach for stabilizing glucose levels in patients.

Here is yet another way that you can cross "the great divide." AEGON Canada Inc., is a financial services company. Fiona Betiviou is their Manager of Training and Development. We spent some time with her after a workshop that Jim had conducted last year in Toronto. Since then, Fiona has made such progress with business partnership initiatives that AEGON Canada Inc. made our list of top ten superstars.

AEGON Canada Inc. Best Practice #1

"The name of the leadership program we ended up developing is 'The Leading Edge.' This program originally had twelve modules because I just kept building more and more sessions. All the Level 1 data were showing me that people loved the sessions, so I kept adding more. Finally, when we began to collect Level 3 data, we found that, while participants may have loved the training, they used only certain modules. I decided that it would be best for us to spend our money on something that is thorough and meaningful and that makes a change to our company."

Fiona simply used her own understanding of the vision for the company, some Level 3 data, and her common sense to make a case for a business partnership effort that would streamline a leadership training program.

The Trainer's Trainer

We cannot end this chapter without turning to one of our key case contributors, Edward Jones, a financial services company in the United States, Canada, and the UK. Strategic Learning Services is the key to their role, and that role is key to how the group facilitates the partnership between training and business objectives.

Edward Jones Best Practices #1

The Strategic Learning Services department does not deliver specific training programs, other than to help make other training departments within Edward Jones more effective. The Strategic Learning Services department provides a strong connection between the many Edward Jones training departments and their business partners.

When interacting with Don, Wendy, and I in a number of instances, we realized that Edward Jones labeled Levels 1 and 2 as "consumptive measures" and Levels 3 and 4 as "impact measures." This means that Levels 1 and 2 are where the money gets spent for training, and Levels 3 and 4 are where the benefits are realized. Edward Jones leveraged these terms to help training and business leaders alike understand that, for key programs, they need to work together in order to both create value for the business and then demonstrate that value.

Beyond Training

After successfully engaging your business leaders to partner with training, it is time to determine to what degree that training is a key element in addressing the business needs or opportunities identified by your stakeholders. We have chosen not to go into detail on this topic, as the literature is replete with models for making this connection. Suffice it to say that it is of critical importance to identify *all* of the factors that will ultimately offer a comprehensive solution. After all, there are few things that are a bigger waste of time and money than additional training when the outcomes indicate a problem with poor execution of critical behaviors after training.

Wendy's Story

We left off with my accepting a newly created position that was half marketing, half training. My new title was Regional Program Manager. I had no idea what a ride I was in for! My new company was culturally very different from my past companies. While it was a large company, it was run like a small proprietorship. Things moved slowly. A vice president gave me the following advice as a new associate: "Learn who owns what turf, and then stay away from it!"

I was encouraged to "train" on my own for many months. There was no push at all for me to make any kind of contribution. For some people, this could be a dream job. For me—a driven person accustomed to fast-paced environments and pressure to produce, produce, produce—it was frankly quite difficult. I did what I could to get out in the field and work with people. I took any opportunity I could to do something that felt like work. And in doing so, I got my first real taste of what a true lack of business partnership feels like.

My first training assignment, if you will, was to visit a sales meeting at our Southwest Division. I presented our sales training program to a group of about fifteen representatives. I really wasn't prepared for what happened next. I gave an overview of the program and highlighted their progress over the previous year. This is where things got a little ugly.

Apparently the training program had been developed in a vac-uum. The training department had designed product training mod-ules with limited involvement from the product managers and none from the sales group (the participants in the training pro-gram). The program was "required" for all of the sales reps regard-less of their level of experience. So reps with twenty-plus years of selling experience were being asked to watch noninteractive e-learning modules on basic product knowledge.

When the sales reps really showed their anger was with the testing at the end of each module. The courses had been designed with no pre-test and no way to "test out" of the course. So, after watching what was described to me as a boring, tedious PowerPoint show, the reps had to pass a ten-question quiz. The questions were multiple choice and true/false, owing to technological limitations. And apparently many of them were grammatically incorrect, con-fusing or intentionally tricky, of limited educational value, and in some cases just plain wrong. So reps who *knew* the products well were being asked to take a faulty quiz to "prove" their knowledge. And they were getting the answers wrong.

Well, no wonder they were a little bit angry. With sympathy, I gathered the comments and delivered them to the training group—where I was met with open arms and open minds, ready to modify the training to meet the needs of the learner, right? *I wish!* No, I was questioned up and down, disbelieved, told I wasn't a team player, and instructed that I should have "set them straight." And this was said by the people in my own training department! Maybe this new job in training and marketing wasn't going to be such a great break, after all.

Key Points

- Start off by making a pledge to partner with your key business leaders and functions.

- Figure out a way to formally discuss this proposed partnership with your potential business partners.

- Strongly consider creating a Learning Council or Advisory Board, made up of training and business people.

- Leverage your new partnership by using your organization's mission, vision, and core values, or by showcasing a high impact program.

- Communicate the point that training, by itself, is rarely a major problem or solution. The most impact comes from what happens after a training program.

5

Step 2: Address Important Jury Issues

"Anyone who stops learning is old, whether at 20 or 80.
Anyone who keeps learning stays young."

—Henry Ford

ONE MIGHT THINK that this chapter should be entitled "Needs Assessments." If that were all there were to this second step, then that is what we would have called the chapter. But, no, this vital second step lays the groundwork for the remainder of the process and is much more than a needs assessment. The work done in this step culminates in the Return on Expectations.SM But to reach that point, you need to understand and *address now* what it is your stakeholders expect you to deliver.

Addressing the training needs of your organization's stakeholders requires an understanding and acknowledgment of your

Kirkpatrick Business Partnership Steps						
P	A	R	T	N	E	R
Pledge	**ADDRESS**	Refine	Target	Necessities	Execute	ROE

Return on Expectations, or ROE. Though this is the name we've given for Step 7 of the model, you need to know its meaning right now.

> ► *Return on Expectations (ROE)*: What your stakeholders expect your training programs or processes to deliver, as well as your ability to demonstrate that you have done so.

There. Enough said. On to Chapter 8.

No, not enough said—not by a long shot. This step is something that almost all learning professionals agree with, and most of them say they do it. But we think otherwise. Rather than assume that you have this step "down pat" and jump to the next chapter, we go into detail here as to how to pull this off.

ROE or ROI?

The term ROI (return on investment) is much more common in the business literature than ROE, but we prefer ROE. A broader term, ROE fits better with our argument that learning professionals tend to be trainer-centered rather than learner-centered or, especially, business-centered. ROI tends to be narrow in its application, too financial for the training situation. Now, don't get us wrong. Talking the language of dollars and cents and the bottom line, and being able to express your value to the business in those terms, is admirable, but it must be done with the specific expectations of your stakeholders—your corporate jury—in mind.

Paul Gregory, Manager of Organizational Development and Employment for the city of Regina, Ontario, gave us his opinion on the usage of ROI and ROE:

"I just don't like ROI," said Gregory. "It is cold, financial, and relevant only to higher-level managers. I *love* ROE. It is a term that everyone can embrace. The [city] employees of Regina can all grasp that, and understand that each of them has expectations from someone—a manager or supervisor, or themselves—and can relate to that. I want to use concepts that everyone can relate to, not just those directly responsible for the bottom line.

"We want all our workers to believe they are ambassadors of the city. As an example, I happened to notice one of our field workers mowing the lawn of a park. A family was having lunch on part of the grass he was to mow. Well, he steered clear of that area until they were done, and he ended up talking with them about the Regina park system. He truly saw his job as not just cutting grass, but also of providing information and being kind to the public. This was his way of creating ROE."

Understanding ROE leads you to what the expectations are of your business partners, and that leads you directly to your corporate jury. While everyone doesn't work in a corporation as such, "corporate jury" is a generic term we use here to describe your key stakeholders, whoever they may be in your organization. So, let's take a closer look at that corporate jury.

The All-Important Jury

Our friend Don Murphy, an attorney in Indianapolis and organizational development specialist, shared with us just how important jury selection and management is in legal cases. In fact, opposing attorneys spend a lot of time and effort trying to get people on the jury who will likely find in their favor. While most often learning professionals do not have the luxury of selecting their corporate jury members, *knowing* who is on your jury is critical.

Juries for civil trials are ordinary citizens who try to make sense of the facts and testimonials they hear, and then they render a judgment. Our corporate juries are not too much different from that. They, too, are ordinary people (well, you may think some of them are not) in positions of influence and authority who will ultimately judge the relative value of the work you do. Therefore, knowing who is on your corporate jury is critical.

Did you know that, for especially important cases, law firms hire jury consultants? These consultants are professionals in the field of psychology who not only assist with jury selection but also carefully observe the jury members during the trial to determine their reactions to different types of questions and various kinds of evidence presented. They then subsequently advise the trial lawyers how to do more of "this" or less of "that." (By the way, some people have suggested that I change my title to Corporate Jury Consultant—not a bad idea!)

Allright, let's talk about identifying your particular corporate jury members. Remember, they are your organization's major stakeholders, the business leaders who ask you for the training programs, the people who provide the input when budget time comes. They are accountable for achieving the business results you are trying to positively impact. They are often the key players in the overall success of your business partnership initiative. They are also your *accusers*, should you not meet their expectations.

And why is it so important that you identify these people and also get to know something about them? There are two reasons. First, they are your source of information for what will become your program's expectations. Have you any idea how common it is for learning professionals to move forward with their programs without a clear idea of what is expected? Without that clear picture you cannot focus your efforts on the development, delivery, and reinforcement of the critical behaviors. Sure, you can create tons of activity, but that is like rolling the dice in Vegas. It is much better to know what is expected, so you can direct your efforts toward meeting those expectations.

The second reason is that these people will be judging whether your efforts have been worth their expense, as they see it. If you know something about them, you can gather your evidence, prepare your report, and present your case in a compelling way.

For instance, if your jury is a CFO, two sales division leaders, and the head of operations, and you determine that three of the four are "just get to the numbers" people, you will want to emphasize the data for all four Kirkpatrick Levels, yet add a testimonial or two for the fourth person, who will more likely be moved by a compelling story of how two leaders worked effectively together. And if you learn that they like handouts and brief slides, you can tailor your presentation of evidence to include those media.

Think of it this way. Many people conduct four-level evaluations on mission-critical projects, and end up with a nice report that they then forward to their bosses or other stakeholders. That is generally not a good idea in and of itself. How effective do you think a trial attorney would be if he merely presented the jury with a printed report on the facts of the case? The *magic* is often in the presentation.

> **Business Partnership Tip:** Do what you can to ensure that jurors are clear about their role in driving the initiative and in passing judgment on its overall value.

A Star with Many Juries

Let's look at some examples from our list.

Edward Jones Best Practice #2

As mentioned in their first best practice, the Strategic Learning Services department was developed to assist the other training functions within Edward Jones. They have a quite diverse jury. First, there are the leaders of those training departments that will need to find the efforts that his team makes worthwhile to them. These people include members of the Financial Advisor (FA) Development Team, the Curriculum Team and the Field Trainers. If they are not convinced that the efforts are worthwhile, they will simply do a 'workaround' and ignore best practices of the Strategic Learning Services. Therefore, Strategic Learning Services creatively finds ways to bring *observable, measureable value* to them. For the most part, they accompish this by helping them to extend their influence beyond the classroom. They show them practical and efficient ways to both create and to then demonstrate that value to the various business partners within Edward Jones.

Second, by doing that, Strategic Learning Services and the other training teams are able to prepare their evidence for that second group of jury members—the *business leaders themselves*. And they have done this by the number one (Kirkpatrick) recommended method: identifying a high impact program, eliciting the partnership effort to ensure it was successful, gathering evidence along the way, and presenting their compelling evidence to the business jury.

The New FA program trains approximately 1500 new students per year on two campuses in separate parts of the country. 100% of the students work in two-person offices or in their own homes. They are the major source of revenue generated by Edward Jones, and, therefore, attract a high amount of interest from all jury members. The New FA Training teams are intimately aware of the interests, tendencies, and the likes/dislikes of their jury members. Does this sound sneaky? Not at all. It is part of the tried and true method of ultimately delivering ROE to the organization. Specifically, these leaders include Visiting Veterans, who are experienced Financial Advisors (FAs), and other area business leaders.

There is a third group of individuals who have a member or two sitting on Strategic Learning Services jury, and they are representatives from IT, HR, and Marketing. While they are also partners in the sense that Strategic Learning Services will not be successful without them (tune in to Chapter 9 for details), they must also be convinced of the value that Strategic Learning Services brings, which in turn will likely cause them to be freer with their future collaboration efforts.

The Edward Jones example may sound a bit complicated, but it is not unlike a trial jury, in that it involves people from different backgrounds with different personalities. To be successful, you must be able to manage multiple expectations. Being a capable learning professional, you will be able to do it.

It is important to note that it is highly unlikely your corporate jury will be the same for every major initiative you bring forth. Sure, some will likely be the same (for example, they may always include the chief operating officer, director of sales, chief financial officer, and perhaps your chief executive officer). But other members of the juries will vary from program to program, as not all business leaders hold the same level of responsibility for every program.

A Star with No Identity Problems

The Allen County Department of Transportation (A-DOT) provides another look at how to identify who is on your corporate jury. With help and guidance of several members of the Human Resources Training and Development Department (HRTDD), we identified their jury members for a major program that was designed to improve the efficiency and effectiveness of highway work zones during resurfacing projects, generally referred to as the "road sealing process."

Allen County Department of Transportation Best Practice #2

According to the staff, HRTDD wanted to increase its influence on the bottom line, including having an overall positive impact on the taxpayers of the county. They also wanted to be able to demonstrate that impact. Recently, they decided to identify a program that would command the interest of senior training and business leaders at A-DOT. They chose a program designed to improve the safety of construction work zones and increase the efficiency of road-sealing operations.

Before they jumped in and started developing and tweaking the training, they decided to identify just who was on their jury—who would be the leaders that would judge the overall impact of the program in relation to time spent and cost. It really wasn't that hard. They came up with the following list for their jury:

- Safety managers

- District engineers

- Traffic control

- Risk managers

- Maintenance supervisors

Not only were these the people who we would have to impress, but they were the people we would need during the reinforcement phases of the program to make it successful.

Take the time to also determine who is on your personal jury. After all, during tough economic times, we learning professionals need to create and demonstrate the value we as individuals bring to a business. The process is the same: Decide to make an impact, and identify the people who will provide your evidence and demonstrate your value.

If you are not sure who is on your jury for a particular program, ask yourself (or someone else), "Who are the people who will be held accountable for the results of this initiative?" Or, "Who are the people who will determine your budget or your staffing in the future?" These are great places to start!

Business Partnership Tip: Ask your organization's key stakeholders to select a showcase program. Have them name one program that is mission-critical to a department or even to the entire organization.

Delicate Jury Issues

Now that you have identified your jury members, it is time to ask for their expectations. Keep in mind that these are expectations of the entire Kirkpatrick Business Partnership Model, played out through the course of the initiative, not the expectations for a training event. This may sound familiar and in a sense you probably are right. But we hope to provide you with some new insights on how to tighten the way you determine stakeholder (jury) expectations.

Our friend from the Netherlands, Diederick Stoel, CEO of Profitwise, Inc., and a training portfolio and evaluation specialist, often talks about "negotiating value propositions." Highlight those three words—they capture the essence of what needs to happen next. As mentioned before, it is unwise, and relatively unproductive, to move ahead with a training initiative unless you are clear about what is expected of you. But finding out what is expected is rarely as easy as crossing the metaphorical bridge and knocking on the doors of your jury members to ask them.

No, unfortunately, they won't always understand what you are asking. Your first clue that this is the case comes when you get an answer like, "We just want all of our leaders to be trained."

> ▶ *Negotiating value propositions:* The act of brainstorming the possibilities, then negotiating and agreeing on expectations that are realistic for you and satisfactory to the jury.

Determining the Expectations

It is quite likely that the jury members just don't know what they truly expect or need from you. Many times, the impetus for a major training or cultural initiative is that "the guy down the street is doing it." You know, it's the flavor-of-the-month thing. For instance, we know of a large hospital network in the eastern United States that decided that its new corporate initiative for 2007 was going to be a program they called "Drive to Excellence." When asked what their specific expectations were for all of the training, software, new processes and systems, projects, and reinforcement that were planned, the senior leaders could only respond, "We'll know it when we see it." When pressed, eight of them finally provided eight different answers. We are still waiting for them to make up their mind, as it would be a poor decision to move ahead before the expected outcome were determined.

Another possibility when the jury seems uncertain of objectives is that the business leaders may have unrealistic expectations. We know of a company that decided to develop and deliver a half-day program on improving self-esteem to all of its nonsupervisory staff. The implicit expectation? To increase market share. We don't know about you, but we would not want to take on that case.

The trick, then, is to brainstorm the possibilities, then negotiate and agree on the expectations, which should be both realistic and satisfy the jury. That's it in a nutshell. But it can be a sticky wicket to get through—and get through, you must. Let us reemphasize here that you do this for major, mission-critical programs, not for every initiative or program you propose. For not only wouldn't you have the resources to do such extensive scouting, but you need to be selective when approaching jury members, lest you wear out your welcome.

So, how do you approach this matter? First, set up a time to talk with key stakeholders about the initiative. Second, do your homework. Here is a list of what you can do ahead of time so that you go into the discussion prepared to offer wise suggestions for overall expectations:

- Review the organization's mission, vision, and key values to find elements that can be converted into relevant expectations.

- Check out your current strategic plan and other corporate directives.

- Benchmark other organizations that have implemented similar initiatives.

- Study any documentation for your initiative and look for any hints of "program intent."

- Talk to people, apart from jury members, who can offer insights into the intent of the program.
- Read books on scorecards and dashboards that will provide ideas (like ASTD's WLP Scorecard).

Now, make a list of what you believe are realistic expectations for the program that may appeal to your jury members. Try to anticipate which expectations they will most likely favor. Finally, make a list of questions you can ask your jury members to determine their expectations. Typical questions are:

- What are you hoping to see happen as a result of this initiative?
- What are your superiors holding you responsible for in light of this effort?
- What key business metrics do you hope to see improve as a result of this initiative?
- What key employee benefits do you hope to see as a result of this initiative?
- How do you envision our customers will benefit from this effort?
- How will our shareholders benefit from this effort?

Types of Jury Expectations

Typically, you can divide the jury's expectations into three basic categories:

1. *Business.* This group of expectations can include increases in revenue, market share, earnings per share, and sales; or decrease in costs, scrap, turnaround time, and so on. You may want to solicit more generic

expectations, like increased productivity, increased profitability, increased brand recognition, happier customers, more satisfied patients, and the like. At this point, do not try to convert these general expectations into specific metrics.

2. *Human Resources.* This group of expectations will likely include results such as increases in retention of key talent, faster promotions, increases in employee engagement, greater attraction of key talent, and so forth. Again, do not try to convert these general goals into specific metrics or measurable amounts of change.

3. *Culture.* These expectations are even more general and are often expressed as increases in team orientation, implementation of a new leadership model, or development of a stronger global presence.

Here's a bit of strong advice: Make sure you get beyond a "training/learning" mindset and think like a business leader. That style of thinking will move you from Level 1 and 2 expectations (e.g., satisfaction with training, competencies realized, skill gaps closed, etc.) and into business strategy-type expectations (engagement, retention, customer satisfaction, revenue, etc.). Remember that most executives do not care about Level 1 and Level 2 indicators. Those are the trainer's job, and for them are merely a means to an end (their expectations).

To move from training expectations to business expectations, do it best with a question: "In order to what?" For instance, suppose the responses you get sound like: "We want all of our leaders trained. We want the classes filled up, and people excited about our new leadership model. And we want them to apply the skills they learned to their jobs." That is *checkmark training.* You must then ask them (or yourself!) the follow-up question: "In order to what?" Keep at it until they (and you) break out of the training-centered world and move up into the world of business. You know you have gotten to where you want to be—and they need to be—when you hear responses like, "In order to increase revenue" or "In order to reduce attrition by twenty percent" or "In order to increase our brand recognition."

> **Business Partnership Tip:** Make sure you move beyond the training/learning mindset and think like a business leader. Follow up generalizations with the question "In order to what?"

When working with your key stakeholders to determine specific program expectations, make sure your "internal consultant hat" is on. Be as helpful as you can be to end up with a list of four, five, or six somewhat generic expectations that will seem realistic and popular with your jury.

"But It's out of My Control"

Many learning professionals shy away from attempting to cross the metaphorical bridge to become strategic business partners. They say, "I really don't want to go there. I will have no control over many of the factors that will affect and impact my contribution. I don't want to be blamed for those things, so I choose to stick with what is within my sphere of control." This is a logical point, yet one that can and needs to be challenged. Doing so introduces the concept of a mitigating factor.

> ▸ *Mitigating factor:* A fact or circumstance associated with a business partnership initiative that, while not an excuse or justification, may reduce its effectiveness.

This is the time for you to explore factors that lay outside of your control and that may adversely affect the outcome of your efforts. These mitigating factors may include market conditions, weather, the economy, and so on. It is wise to point them out early on, so that your jury will take them into consideration at the proper time.

> **Business Partnership Tip:** Extend your role beyond what you have control over. Push the importance of influence over control.

Here is another important tip. Your stakeholders will likely not think of every possible or likely positive outcome from a proposed program or initiative. Bring your internal or external consultant cadre of skills along with you to these discussions, and be prepared to offer additional benefits if they do not come up in conversation. These benefits may include greater employee engagement and retention, especially strong points when dealing with highly business-minded jury members.

Jury Expectations in Relation to the Four Levels

Why are jury expectations so important in relation to the Kirkpatrick Four Levels? Consider an example. Let's say an organization we'll call Dena Consulting Service is asked to conduct in-house programs on generational employees for three companies. How should Dena proceed? Can they present the same material for all three? Not necessarily. If they first ask each company, "What are your expectations?" they will be better able to determine the type of training to provide and determine the required follow-up to manifest those accomplishments and meet the company's expectations.

Let's say Company A says, "We want our people to be aware of and have a good appreciation and understanding of the different generations of employees." Company B says, "We want our participants to be able to conduct effective development activities for each generation." Company C says, "We want to see improvement in engagement scores and subsequent improvement in retention of top talent for each generational employee group." Table 5-1 shows the three responses and the Kirkpatrick level required in order to achieve positive ROE.

It is hoped that Table 5-1 shows how different answers to the question of expectations guide the focus and level of effort required.

TABLE 5-1.   Three Companies and Three Levels of Effort

Company	Expectation	Kirkpatrick Level	Level of Effort for Consultant	Level of Effort for Company
A	"Be aware of and have a good appreciation and understanding of generational differences."	Level 1 Level 2	Develop and deliver a basic program on generational differences	Get people to show up and learn
B	"Conduct effective developmental activities for each genera-tional employee group."	Level 1 Level 2 Level 3	Develop and deliver training and develop-ment programs that effectively impact each generation	Reinforce the training coach for effective training of all generations
C	"Improve engagement and retention of each genera-tional group."	Level 1 Level 2 Level 3 Level 4	Full-blown KBPM implementation	Full-blown KBPM implementation

As another example of varying levels of effort, consider this: One of our clients is the Abu Dhabi Police Department in the United Arab Emirates. The department members are eager learners, interested in applying the principles of the KBPM in an effort to ensure safe, efficient, and pleasant surroundings for the residents and tourists. I met with Major Abdulla, who is in charge of the Evaluation Department. While talking about our work together, and his expectations, we came up with five such expectations:

1. Make Level 1 forms more learner-centered, and increase the rate of response in remote locations.
2. Develop a Level 2 methodology that emphasizes credible yet cost-effective pre- and post-assessments.
3. Develop a Level 3 methodology that highlights surveys and observation/feedback.
4. Successfully link Level 3 into performance appraisals.
5. Create exceptional value for the business and demonstrate it (Level 4).

Note that these expectations are in a generally nonmeasurable form, which is both fine and correct. In the next step, these general expectations are converted to measurable, targeted outcomes.

Our Stars and Their Jury Expectations

Table 5-2 shows the early jury expectations for three of the stars highlighted in this book.

In the next chapter we consider one of the most significant and oft-ignored steps in the KBPM: converting your jury's expectations into observable, measurable Level 3 and Level 4 outcomes.

TABLE 5-2.   Showcase Programs and Jury Expectations for Three Stars

Star	Showcase Program	Corporate Jury Expectations
Allen County Department of Transportation	Road Sealing Process	1. Training costs are reduced. 2. Road sealing is done cost effectively. 3. Roads are improved effectively. 4. The overall evaluation process be replicated throughout A-DOT.
Georgia-Pacific Consumer Products	Managing Remote Team Members	1. Demonstrate program-learned skills on the job. 2. Become a highly effective remote team leader. 3. Create a positive impact on the customer.
Region of Waterloo	Learning to Lead	1. Leaders increase their self-awareness. 2. Leaders initiate and implement change. 3. Leaders foster a citizen-centered culture. 4. Leaders build and maintain internal and external relationships. 5. Leaders achieve organizational objectives. 6. Leaders motivate and develop people. 7. Leaders are politically and organizationally sensitive.

Wendy's Story

At the end of the last chapter I had my first taste of the conflict between the training team and the audience for their programs. While it was a lucky break for me to get a job where I could learn about training, it was quickly becoming obvious that perhaps the reason this company would allow someone with no training experience to do training is that the staff were not experts in it themselves. I knew that I would not want to learn how to do training from a company that did not even include the target audience in its needs assessment and design process! And that was before I even knew what a needs assessment was!

I set out to find some good, solid training knowledge. I attended a six-day instructional design program for certification. I also got certified to facilitate three outside programs, figuring that they would be good models for delivering training. I read books as fast as I could. I made a point of connecting with outside consultants and trainers to ask their advice. I created my own, informal "training advisory board." I soaked in all the knowledge I could obtain.

This was both a happy and an anxiety-filled time in my career. The more I learned about training, the more I saw the tremendous business value it could have if done right. I felt as if I had found my true calling. My business background (and initial skepticism about the value of training) made the perfect foundation for a career in executing training that would create value and make a difference. I had a compulsion like never before to continue to learn and do as much training as I could to practice my newfound knowledge.

But the happiness in my discovery process was tempered by anxiety. The more I learned about training, the more I could see that many people around me did not share the same discipline. Much of the training produced by my company was not developed using the ADDIE model, or any design model that I could see. The training department sometimes had an arrogance that they "knew best." On the rare occasions when they collected evaluation data, they often ignored it. "The learners don't really know what they need" was a common phrase during planning meetings. Or, "Yes, we can see that some people have requested that we change our training, but you can't please everyone so we are going to continue to do it the way we know is best." It was both a frustrating and an embarrassing time to be the liaison between the learners and a training-centric organization. I didn't believe in pedagogical, trainer-centric training. Yet I knew that if I could move the needle and create training more in line with learner needs, I could have a huge impact.

So, I had a decision to make. Could I stay in the company that I felt really didn't "get it," so that I would have the opportunity to continue my self-education in training? Could I stand to be part of something I really didn't believe in if I could stay focused on the horizon?

Key Points

- Return on Expectations (ROE) is an all-inclusive way of positioning how you will add value to your organization's bottom line.

- It is critical to know your corporate jury so you will later know how to deliver your evidence to them in the most compelling manner possible.

- It is important to negotiate expectations, not just ask your jury members what they are.

- It is critical to reach beyond your areas of control (Levels 1 and 2) into your areas of influence (Levels 3 and 4) to create value.

6

Step 3: Refine Expectations to Define Outcomes

"Yes we can. Yes we will. If we all work together."
—BARACK OBAMA, 2009 PRESIDENTIAL ACCEPTANCE SPEECH

WE ARE EXCITED that you are reading this chapter, as the principles herein have been especially helpful to learning professionals, from individual consultants to CLOs, and everyone in between. Here, we move to the third step of the Kirkpatrick Business Partnership Model (KBPM).

Clear Expectations Lead to Sharp Focus

The clearer you are about what is expected of you, the more focused your efforts. This is true in almost any endeavor,

Kirkpatrick Business Partnership Steps						
P	A	R	T	N	E	R
Pledge	Address	**REFINE**	Target	Necessities	Execute	ROE

whether writing job descriptions, providing performance appraisals, taking college exams, doing household chores (Jim knows personally about this one), maintaining personal relationships, or developing learning initiatives. Here, you take the good work you did in Step 2 and sharpen the focus to be able to meet the expectations of stakeholders. Specifically, you will convert the general expectations you gathered previously into observable, measurable Level 3 and Level 4 outcomes. This is when you lay the foundation for adding incredible value to your organization.

> **Business Partnership Tip:** The clearer you are about what is expected of you, the more focused you can make your efforts.

We are going to give away a bit of the farm here before getting to the details of this step. We want you to know three phrases that will prove useful when you complete this step of the KBPM:

- "What will success look like?"
- "Leading to what?"
- "In order to . . . ?"

Mike Woodard from Georgia-Pacific Consumer Products is passionate about serving his business partners. Here's a phone conversation Jim had with him that illustrates how these three phrases can be used. While Jim knew that *he* knew the answers to the questions before he asked them, Mike humored Jim by responding typically.

> JIM: Hi, Mike. . . . Can we talk about your "Managing Remote Team Members" program for a few minutes?
>
> MIKE: Sure. What do you want to know?
>
> JIM: I understand that this program is part of a two-year developmental journey for these leaders. What else can you tell me about it?
>
> MIKE: The actual training event is one day, but we have lots of pre-positioning activities and, of course, intense follow-up. Here are some of the things we are doing. . . .
>
> JIM: Great. What will you want participants to be able to do as a result of going through the program?
>
> MIKE: We want them to develop strong listening skills, collaborate better, handle difficult situations more effectively, reach out to employees professionally and in friendship, and generally become effective remote team leaders.
>
> JIM: I understand that you have a corporate [business] sponsor for this initiative. In order to get to the all-important business perspective, I would like to ask you the "in order to what" questions and have you answer from her perspective. Okay?
>
> MIKE: Sure. Shoot.
>
> JIM: The targeted objectives of this program will allow participants to be able to develop strong listening skills, collaborate better, handle difficult situations more effectively, reach out to employees profession-

ally and in friendship, and generally become effective remote team leaders. My question is, that is all well and good, but what are those behaviors, when consistently applied, designed to bring about *from a business perspective*? Or, saying it another way, they are to be practiced on the job *in order to . . . what*?

MIKE: In order to accomplish their day-to-day tasks more efficiently.

JIM: In order to . . . ?

MIKE: . . . get orders and back orders processed accurately and on time, and for the employees to feel better about the job they do. . . .

JIM: In order to . . . ?

MIKE: . . . increase customer and employee satisfaction.

JIM: In order to . . . ?

MIKE: . . . increase revenue, realize cost savings, increase employee engagement, and increase retention of our key people. Now stop bothering me!

Well, he may not have made the final remark, but some of your jury members may feel badgered when you question them like this. Make sure you reinforce the idea that this questioning will ultimately serve their important business objectives,

Do you see how you have moved from the training world to the business world? While clarifying the business expectations for the training initiative, you'll also be setting yourself up for a successful conclusion.

Business Partnership Tip: Use the "in order to . . ." response to move from tactical, training-focused thinking to business-strategy thinking.

You can also see from this example that it is much easier to attach metrics to Mike's final thoughts than it would be for their initial ones, which were Level 3 behaviors. This great news counters the argument we hear all the time: "Level 4 is too hard!" Well, guess what? Mike determined the key Level 4 metrics already being tracked by his company. (If you didn't highlight the last statement of that phone conversation, please do so, as it will save you lots of time later on.)

Managing Jury Expectations Along the Way

It is critically important to manage the expectations of the jury while the training program is executed. One of the best ways to do this is to send them a dashboard or mini-scorecard on a monthly basis that includes both Level 3 and Level 4 metrics. Once your outcomes have been defined, it's easy to see what information should be included. If we revisit our courtroom metaphor, this compares to the defense attorney presenting bits of evidence along the way, prior to making the closing argument.

"What Will Success Look Like?"

Linda Hainlen, from Clarian Health, one of our KBPM superstars, uses the question, "What will success look like?" when she initially meets with her internal clients. Here is what she has to say about it.

Clarian Health Best Practice #2

Beginning with the end in mind sounds easy, but can have its challenges. We were recently asked to train approximately 3,000 nurses on a computer program that helps stabilize glucose levels. When I met with the administrator who requested the training and I asked what I could do for her, she stated, "I need you to train approximately 3,000 nurses on X program by X date."

That answer didn't really tell me what *success* would look like. So I asked what she really wanted me to *accomplish*. She stated: "I need you to train approximately 3,000 nurses on X program by X date." At the risk of being annoying, I probed further. I finally asked, "Why are we doing this?" She responded,

"I learned that many of our patients who are admitted into our hospital for various reasons are also diabetic. While focusing on treating the life-threatening symptoms that brought these patients to the hospital, [we found that their] glucose levels could become unstable. Maintaining glucose levels within a designated range is extremely important to ensure the safety of the patient."

Thus, the tool we were asked to train the staff on would help monitor and stabilize glucose levels, ensure a safer passage for the patient, and therefore ensure better patient safety and outcomes. And *that* was what success would look like to those "jury members." If your jury members are not accustomed to being asked for their expectations, you may have to assist them in defining exactly what they believe success looks like.

Let's now look at a simple example: the work-zone example at Allen County Department of Transportation (A-DOT) that was presented in the last chapter. Table 6-1 summarizes the members of the jury, their expectations, and the answer to the question, "What will success look like?"

We don't know about you, but we surely would not want to target the training to or measure the success against the jury expectations as given in the middle column. Whether you agree with what they came up with or not, at least the elements in the last column are measurable and, therefore, a good place to plant

TABLE 6-1. A-DOT Jury Expectations and Targeted Outcomes

Jury Members	Jury Expectations	Targeted Outcomes ("What will success look like?")
• Safety managers • District engineers • Traffic control • Risk managers • Maintenance supervisors	1. Smooth traffic flow 2. Increased safety for workers and motorists in highway work zones 3. Better planning	1. Less than 15-minute delays 2. Reduction in injuries and fatalities 3. Increase in projects completed on time and on budget

your flags in the ground. They are solid, measurable outcomes from a training, reinforcement, and Level 4 perspective.

Let's refer back to Table 5-1, showing the expectations of companies A, B, and C for a generational development program. Now, Table 6-2 shows how these expectations might be converted to "What would success look like?" outcomes.

How Far Can You Move the Needle?

The above example brings up a crucial decision that you must make. We like to refer to this process of targeting the outcomes as "identifying the needles" for the metrics that you believe the initiative will move. That is, there is always the question, "Should I include the targeted *amount* of change—an increase or decrease—that is expected to occur?" The answer is, maybe. We strongly suggest that you do so if you are reasonably confident in the numbers. And we suggest that you don't if you are not sure of those numbers. Targeting the *proper* metrics is the critical point here; being an accurate forecaster is not. Remember: You don't want to promise something you cannot be rea-

TABLE 6-2. Three Companies with Three Targeted Outcomes

Company	Jury Expectation	Kirkpatrick Level	Targeted Outcomes
A	"Be aware of and have a good appreciation and understanding of generational differences."	Level 2	1. 95% attendance of invited employees. 2. 4.5 or above on key Level 1 indicators. 3. 90% of participants pass post-test.
B	"Conduct effective developmental activities for each generational employee group."	Level 3	1. Participants work on teams to develop and facilitate a program for managers detailing generational differences and implications. 2. Each participant incorporates relevant generational learning methods into one major ongoing program.
C	"Improve engagement and retention of each generational group."	Level 4	1. Improved employee engagement scores across the generations. 2. Improved retention of top talent across the generations.

sonably sure can be achieved. Our advice: under-promise and over-deliver.

In summary, if you are confident in and have access to specific metrics and their likely movement, use them. If not, phrase the outcomes of your initiative in terms of "increase" or "decrease," without stating a specific amount of change. Just make sure that you understand the goals of your business stakeholders—your jury members—so that these will be your ultimate indicators of success.

What if you are not sure about any metrics for your training program at all? Then, as a good trial lawyer knows, go with the subjective. Go with the testimonials. We talk more about this in Chapter 10.

Finding Measurable Outcomes

To further illustrate how to convert general expectations into measurable outcomes, Table 6-3 summarizes the stakeholder expectations and outcomes identified for the Abu Dhabi Police Department project, mentioned in the last chapter.

Note again that the measurable outcomes need not be limited to financial or human resource results. They can address any of the four levels. This allows for clear focus on pre-training, training, and post-training efforts. And, as a bonus, it helps training managers to prioritize initiatives not only in terms of time but also resources. If the expectations and desired outcomes only reach Level 1 or 2, save your resources (and your money!) for those that extend to Levels 3 and 4.

Finally, let's revisit a few of the stars and see how they converted expectations into measurable outcomes (see Table 6-4).

Note that some of the targeted outcomes have specific numeric targets and some don't. As stated earlier, if you are confident with the metrics, go with them. If not, it's perfectly fine to just indicate what will be measured.

Note also that some of the outcomes are Level 3 and some are Level 4. As with Step 2, make sure you go into meetings where expectations and success indicators are discussed with specific ideas and recommendations in mind. One of the main reasons trainers are on trial today is that they have not done a

TABLE 6-3.   Abu Dhabi Police Department Expectations and Outcomes

General Stakeholder Expectation ("What are you expecting from this initiative?")	Outcomes
1. Make Level 1 forms more learner-centered and to increase the rate of response in remote locations.	• Develop and pilot new Level 1 survey by November 1. • Increase response-rate average to 90% for paper-and-pencil-based surveys and 40% for electronic surveys.
2. Develop a Level 2 methodology that emphasizes credible yet cost-effective pre- and post-assessments.	• Develop and pilot a new Level 2 assessment template by December 1. • Determine savings generated during pilot.
3. Develop a Level 3 methodology that highlights surveys and observation and feedback.	• Develop and pilot new Level 3 survey and administrative methodology by February 1 of next year. • Develop and pilot new Level 3 observation/feedback form by February 1 of next year.
4. Successfully link Level 3 with performance appraisals.	• Develop and pilot methodology for linking Level 3 data with performance appraisals by April 1 of next year. • Achieve 50% linkage by June 1 of next year. • Achieve 75% linkage within the next two years. • Achieve 100% linkage by December 1 of next year.
5. Create exceptional value for the business and demonstrate it.	• Develop and pilot dashboard template by April 1 of next year. • Achieve 50% application of dashboards by June 1 of next year. • Achieve 100% application of dashboards by December 1 of next year.

TABLE 6-4.   Three Stars Convert Expectations to Targeted Outcomes

Corporate Jury Expectations	Targeted Outcomes
Edward Jones, "New Financial Advisor Program"	

1. High program graduation rate
2. Successfully execute the "Twenty Mile March"
3. Achieve health for and productivity from our new FAs
	1. Graduation rate
	2. Meet the firm's growth goals
	3a. Trainee attrition
	  b. Graduates meet commission standards at 4 months following training
	  c. Graduates place an order within time standards

Allen County Department of Transportation, "Road Sealing Process"	
1. Training costs are reduced. 2. Chip sealing is done cost-effectively. 3. Roads are improved effectively. 4. The overall evaluation process be replicated throughout A-DOT.	1. Cost of training per trainee is reduced 2. District costs decrease by 10% 3a. Percentage of seals holding after 3 months increases b. Percentage of seals holding after 12 months increases 4. Number of users outside HRTDD increases
Georgia-Pacific Consumer Products, "Managing Remote Team Members"	

1. Demonstrate program-learned skills on the job.
2. Become a highly effective remote team leader.
3. Create a positive impact to the customer.
	1. Percentage of positive Level 3 responses increases
	2a. Increase in orders processed on time.
	  b. Decrease in time to fill back orders.
	  c. Increase in direct reports' engagement scores
	3. Increase in customer satisfaction scores

good enough job expanding the role of training, or of its influence in and value to the business. Learning professionals need to act as *trusted advisors* to their business partners, and offering solid suggestions is one way to do that.

Once you have gone through the collaborative process of converting stakeholder expectations into targeted outcomes, check with all of the stakeholders to ascertain that you have captured what they find compelling. A good way to do this is to ask, "Will you be convinced of the value that we bring to the bottom line if we demonstrate positive movement of these success indicators?" If the answer is yes, you are ready to move forward. If not, back up until you receive such assurance.

Key Points

- The clearer you are about what is expected of you, the more focused your efforts can be.

- Three important phrases that are helpful in converting expectations to targeted outcomes are: "What will success look like?" "Leading to what?" and "In order to . . . ?"

- Include the targeted degree of change when defining the outcome only if you are confident that the amount of change is achievable. If not, just define the measurable outcome, without attaching a numeric goal.

- Be prepared to act as an internal consultant as you clarify and agree on the targeted outcomes.

- Remember: moving the needles on your stakeholders' key metrics is ultimately what you are in business to do.

7

Step 4: Target Critical Behaviors and Required Drivers

"Opportunities are usually disguised as hard work,
so most people don't recognize them."
—ANN LANDERS

THIS IS PROBABLY the step that will allow you to rise to a new level of training success. If you are an individual consultant or practitioner, it will provide you with a differentiator that will blow away your competition. So, let's take another look at the Kirkpatrick Business Partnership Model, this time for Step 4.

Kirkpatrick Business Partnership Steps						
P	**A**	**R**	**T**	**N**	**E**	**R**
Pledge	Address	Refine	**TARGET**	Necessities	Execute	ROE

Critical Behaviors

It is important to identify—with the help of line managers (aka the KBPM in action)—the few critical behaviors that training graduates must be able to perform on the job to bring about the targeted outcomes. More is not better here. Keep the assignment as simple as possible here, for two reasons. First, it is important not to confuse employees about which behaviors are the ones that are most likely to bring about success for them in terms of performance and career advancement, and for the organization and its customers. These are the behaviors they should focus on as part of the training. Second, it is important not to overwhelm the supervisors who are going to monitor these new behaviors to ensure that they are adopted. And, believe me, it is not in anyone's best interest to give supervisors more work than they can handle. But, first, let's define the term *critical behaviors*.

> ► *Critical behaviors*: The few, key behaviors that employees will have to consistently perform in order to bring about the targeted outcomes.

Recently we talked with two colleagues from a major children's toy and clothing distributor who provided us with a fine example with which to discuss critical behaviors. The initiative for which the distributor is using the KBPM addresses the goal of decreasing injuries in their warehouses while maintaining efficiencies. The colleagues did a good job converting the stakeholder expectations to measurable targeted outcomes, as evidenced by the initiative's stated goals. As we talked, the colleagues identified the following four critical behaviors:

1. Maintaining three points of contact when climbing
2. Proper setup and use of ladders
3. Following proper procedures when wearing safety equipment
4. Documenting any safety violations

Warehouse employees have been trained to be competent in these and other safety-related procedures. They were also given a safety manual to study and follow. But guess what? Human nature being what it is, these procedures and competencies will not occur naturally and regularly on the job. Research provided by Sandy Almeida, senior consultant and evaluation research and practice expert, shows that, while there are decent correlations between Levels 1 and 2 behaviors, and between Levels 3 and 4, there are no strong correlations between Levels 2 and 3.

This is important to note. Even if skills are learned, people are not likely to apply what they learn on the job without reinforcement and support. Thus, we have the need for organizational drivers.

Just What Are Drivers?

Let's review the definition of drivers, introduced in Chapter 3:

> ► *Required drivers*: Processes and systems that reinforce actions, monitor procedures, and encourage or reward performance of critical behaviors on the job.

Don Kirkpatrick and I (Jim) wrote a book in 2005 called *Transferring Learning to Behavior*. The major theme of that book was that training, in and of itself, is of little value unless participants apply what they learn. We believed that then. We believe it now. This step in the KBPM is about what has to happen *after* a learning intervention that will ensure the behavior is applied in the workplace. Thus, this chapter concerns itself with the required drivers for the program's ultimate success.

> **Business Partnership Tip:** Training, in and of itself, is of little value unless participants apply what they learn.

Your job, thus, in Step 4 is to identify the few critical behaviors that, if implemented effectively over time, will cause the targeted outcomes to result. We often say, "If you do a good job with Levels 1, 2, and 3, Level 4 will take care of itself." The same principle holds true here. Finding the right drivers goes a long way toward bringing success—and, ultimately, a positive verdict from your jury.

We coined the term *missing link* to describe Level 3 of the Kirkpatrick Model. It seems as though trainers are concerned about Levels 1 and 2; business leaders focus on the critical Level 4 outcomes; and nobody takes ownership of Level 3. Yet in a broader sense, this is what Level 3 is all about. In this case, the required drivers are the missing link between the learning events and the business results.

Returning to our example, we see that the children's toy and clothing distributor added drivers they believed would reinforce the critical behaviors that would lead to their targeted outcomes. These drivers are:

1. Supervisors monitor compliance using observation, feedback, and coaching.
2. Publicized consequences for safety violations.
3. Positive reinforcement and support for proper behaviors.
4. Regular checking of safety equipment.

Putting Your Flag in the Ground

Here is where we leave the traditional view of training (the three Ds—designing, developing, and delivering), and we enter a world that is closer to organizational development. This is where you have decided which initiatives are going to provide your stakeholders with the greatest benefit, and you have chosen to muster some serious resources. It is where you put your flag in the ground and say, "This is my significant effort. It will pay off!"

What you want to ensure now is that there is follow-up after your learning intervention that helps people apply what they just learned. The procedure for this follow-up is formalized in your establishment of critical behaviors and required drivers. To give you a better idea of what we mean, here are some examples of common drivers. Note that some drivers are behaviors, some are processes, and some are incentives:

- Coaching to reinforce the skills

- Peer accountability

- Recognition when things are done the right way

- Incentives to reinforce proper application of skills and/ or subsequent results

- Level 3 evaluations

- Monitoring systems—for example, "This call may be recorded for coaching and development purposes"

- Cross-functional review meetings (to monitor behavior trends and outcome progress)

- Action-based learning

- Monitoring action plans

As is the case with critical behaviors, more is not better. The idea is to pick the few drivers that will encourage the most application of learned behaviors and, therefore, the best results. Having too many drivers becomes unmanageable and confuses the participants and their supervisors, especially in regard to which behaviors should command the most attention.

> **Business Partnership Tip:** More is *not* better here. Pick the few drivers that will encourage the most application and, therefore, the best results.

The Kirkpatrick Business Partnership Model really comes to life in this step because both the learning professionals and the business people must share the responsibility of determining these drivers and *making sure that they are used.* (The actual monitoring and mutual accountability takes place during Step 6, so be sure to stay tuned!)

Business Partnership Tip: Hold fast to this principle: Identify only a few key drivers, then monitor them and do whatever is necessary to keep their levels at or above standards.

Confirm the Scope of the Initiative

As you identify the critical behaviors and required drivers, be sure to keep the scope of the initiative in check. Are you familiar with the term "scope creep"? It is not the title of a horror movie, nor is it what happens when good mouthwash goes bad. No, it is making sure that once the scope of a project or program has been defined, that project or program does not wander beyond its boundaries. Of course, you need to make sure the scope of the project is broad enough to ensure that the targeted outcomes can be realized, yet the objectives are manageable and achievable by the participants and their managers.

> ▸ *Scope creep:* When the boundaries of a project or program move beyond those determined during the initial stages.

Here is an example of scope creep. Jim worked with a call center that received a corporate directive to increase customer satisfaction scores. The success outcomes were agreed upon and converted to success outcomes that focused exclusively on those scores. During the time that the critical behaviors and drivers were being selected, it was decided by members of the management team that it would also be nice to track average call time, new orders, and engagement and retention of employees. While these Level 4 results *might* improve as a result of the overall initiative, the training team was going down the path of focusing on customer satisfaction and the type and amount of training and reinforcement that would be needed to improve it.

It would be fine to include the additional metrics in the targeted Level 3 and 4 categories, but it would take a significant amount of additional level of effort, from all parties, to do so, and would need to be renegotiated.

Similarly, we have seen many instances in which a brief training program, in and of itself, was expected to lead to significant positive outcomes. Among these misguided efforts were:

- A two-day sales training course emphasizing product knowledge, designed to significantly increase sales

- A one-day diversity training course, designed to increase the "sensitivity" of attendees

- A two-day in-house, four-level evaluation program, designed to increase profitability

- A four-module e-learning training program, designed to significantly increase customer satisfaction

The important point here is this: while the discussions of these topics should take place early in a training program, the scope of the projects must be sufficiently broad to bring about the outcomes that will meet the expectations of your jury. At the risk of sounding like a broken record, no training event is strong enough to stand alone and bring about significant outcomes. As you progress through the KBPM, make sure that the initiative you are leading contains all the necessary elements of preparation, training, and follow-up to do the job. And if more training components or elements of reinforcement and accountability are required to bring about those desired outcomes, make sure you negotiate for them.

Business Partnership Tip: No training event is strong enough to stand alone and bring about significant outcome.

For example, when we are asked to conduct a two-hour session on evaluating the company's existing training programs, and the expectation of our "jury" is that it will significantly impact their bottom line, we say something like, "Sure. We can do that if we work together. How about if we talk about the processes that will bring that about, such as pre-positioning the learners, creating a way for supervisors to reinforce the behaviors, and providing accountability measures to ensure that the learning gets transferred to on-the-job behavior?"

Once expectations are determined, along with critical behaviors and required drivers, a "level of effort" conversation is indicated. It is a great time to discuss and agree upon who will take responsibility for what is in order to ensure success.

Harder Than It Appears

Within the KBPM, Step 4 can be a challenge, and there are a few reasons that this is so. First, it takes discipline, and being the "quick answer or else" society that we are, taking the high road by making a sustained effort and showing discipline is far from popular. Executives and managers want fast results, and often they lack the patience for a steady reinforcement process to bring about long-term, sustainable results. Second, learning professionals and business leaders alike still believe that the magic is in the training *event*, though by now you recognize that it is only part of the story. Third, it is hard to get people to commit to Level 3 stuff, since typically no group in a business takes responsibility for this phase. So, it is necessary to ask the business supervisors and managers for help. Unfortunately, unless you have made a good business case for what is in it for them (e.g., getting their critical goals achieved), they will likely turn you away and tell you to go back to "where you belong."

Here is how Mike Woodard, at Georgia-Pacific Consumer Products, gains commitment to this process.

Georgia-Pacific Consumer Products Best Practice #2

"I like to use what I call a 'Learning Contract.' Perhaps I should call it a 'Performance Partnership Contract' because it is all about . . . an agreement between Learning and the business [leaders] to ensure that drivers are agreed upon and responsibilities for carrying out each one are determined. I always provide a good business case for why this is critical to the success of the organization. This is especially important for major initiatives with major expectations. If, for instance, my business sales director wants strong results, I must negotiate for strong efforts with drivers.

"We may get a little more formal than most, but we do type out an agreement and all sign it, committing . . . that we will be responsible for our parts of the business partnership model follow-up. If the numbers go below specifications, we have permission to get after one another about them."

▶ *Contract:* An agreement between two or more parties, made orally or in writing, the purpose of which is to create mutual accountability.

In the last chapter, we related part of a conversation that Mike and Jim had about the "Managing Remote Team Members" initiative at Georgia-Pacific. Here are the last few bits of that conversation, with some added dialogue as we continued the conversation about required drivers.

JIM: The targeted objectives for this program will allow participants to be able to develop strong listening skills, collaborate better, handle difficult situations more effectively, reach out to employees professionally and in friendship, and generally become effective remote team leaders. That is all well and good, but what are those behaviors, when consistently applied, designed to bring about from a business perspective? Or, saying it another way, they are to be practiced on the job *in order to what?*

MIKE: In order to accomplish their day-to-day tasks more efficiently.

JIM: In order to . . . ?

MIKE: Get orders and back orders processed accurately and on time, and for the employees to feel better about the job they do.

JIM: In order to . . . ?

MIKE: Increase customer and employee satisfaction.

JIM: In order to . . . ?

MIKE: Increase revenue, employee engagement, and retention of our key people. To realize cost savings.

JIM: Mike, can I ask how you can be sure that the training you provide is going to lead to the outcomes you have mentioned? I mean, this stuff doesn't happen by magic.

MIKE: I'm glad you asked that question [he says that frequently]. We identified the factors, behaviors, and processes that have to be consistently followed *after* training to make sure the behaviors happen, which will lead to the targeted results. I believe you call them "drivers." Then we decided who would be responsible for making sure they do occur, and how we will monitor them.

JIM: Can you give me a handle on what they are?

MIKE: Sure. First, the graduates will be required to journal their coaching and new leadership behaviors.

They will share this journal with their supervisors and with us in the Georgia-Pacific University. Second, we will provide four half-day coaching events for each graduate. The first two will be in person at their site, and the second two will be remote. Third, their KPIs will be tracked, and, if needed, assistance provided by their manager. We believe that these are the three key ongoing drivers that need to occur in order for us to achieve our desired results.

JIM: Thanks, Mike.

We think that the best way to drive this point home is with another example and not a lot of narrative. Here is the Allen County Department of Transportation (A-DOT) example of the agreement on training to help improve the effectiveness and efficiency of road-repair work zones. In Table 7-1, we have expanded the table presented in Chapter 6 to include critical behaviors and required drivers.

TABLE 7-1. A-DOT Expectations, Outcomes, Behaviors, and Drivers

Jury Expectations	Targeted Outcomes	Critical Behaviors	Drivers
1. Smooth traffic flow 2. Increased safety for workers and motorists in highway work zones 3. Better planning	1. Less than 15-minute delays 2. Reduction in injuries and fatalities 3. Increase in projects completed on time and on budget	1. Written work zone plans 2. Plans communicated to public 3. Proper work zone setup 4. Flaggers follow proper procedures	1. Observation, feedback, and coaching by supervisors 2. Ongoing compliance tracking 3. Ongoing execution of formal and informal recognition programs

Note that the critical behaviors are skills being applied on the job by training participants from various departments; the required drivers are what others in the organization need to attend to in order to ensure that these critical behaviors actually are adopted. Thus, the key required drivers "drive" the critical behaviors, and the critical behaviors lead to the targeted outcomes.

> **Business Partnership Tip:** Make the wisest use of your resources. When expectations end at Level 2, there are no drivers necessary because there are no expectations for behavior change or subsequent results. So, save your time and money for other initiatives, programs, and processes where there *is* the expectation for behavior change and results.

Follow the Stars

Now, let's have an expanded look at the stars we highlighted in the last chapter. This time, in Table 7-2, we add the critical behaviors and required drivers.

Earning and Keeping Their Stars

Earlier in this chapter we mentioned customer and patient satisfaction scores. Jim saw this effort alive and well when he stopped into a Cracker Barrel restaurant outside of Indianapolis a few months ago. While he was waiting for a table, being seated, and then being served, he noticed that the employees wore white aprons with one or more silver stars embroidered along the top. His hostess had two stars, and his server and cashier both had

TABLE 7-2.   Three Stars—Their Critical Behaviors and Required Drivers

Targeted Outcomes	Critical Behaviors	Required Drivers
Edward Jones, "New Financial Advisor Program"		
1. Graduation rate 2. Meet the firm's growth goals 3a. Trainee attrition b. Graduates meet commission standards at 4 months following training c. Graduates place an order within time standards	1. Make in-person contact with prospective clients 2. Establish relationships with prospective clients 3. Identify financial needs of customers by asking financial questions 4. Be prepared to offer solutions to prospective clients that meet their financial needs; this critical behavior cannot be executed until the end of the program	1. Awards for prospecting 2. Reinforcement of the culture of sharing and volunteering 3. Peer networking 4. Monitoring of critical behaviors 5. On-the-job training period and related coaching
Allen County Department of Transportation "Road Sealing Process"		
1. Cost of training per trainee 2. District costs decrease by 10% 3a. Percentage of seals holding after 3 months b. Percentage of seals holding after 12 months 4. Number of users outside HRTDD	1. Proper determinations of which roads to seal. 2. Laying down road seals only when weather conditions are suitable. 3. Employees follow proper safety procedures. 4. Employees follow proper sealing processes.	1. Monitoring to see that managers are teaching the principles on the job 2. Level 3 evaluation—surveys, interviews, questionnaires—by HRTDD 3. "Partners-in-the-Field" program 4. HRTDD going to sites to coach and reinforce correct methodology
Georgia-Pacific Consumer Products "Managing Remote Team Members"		
1. Percentage of positive Level 3 responses 2a. Increase in orders processed on time b. Decrease in time to fill back orders c. Increase in direct reports engagement scores 3. Increase in customer satisfaction scores	1. Leaders conduct bi-weekly 1:1's with remote employees. 2. Leaders conduct weekly group meetings with area employees. 3. Leaders complete coaching and KPI logs. 4. Leaders post follow-up action steps to all participants.	1. Multitiered competency program* 2. Targeted meetings with all partners and corporate sponsor 3. Four coaching sessions 4. Peer partnership program 5. Monitoring of key behaviors and performance KPIs

*Upper tiers are gained only through documented application of competencies on the job. This is also linked to pay and promotability.

three stars. He asked his server, "Hey, what's up with the stars?" She replied,

"I earned those stars by passing tests . . . tests about the menu, carrying food, greeting people, and delivering friendly service to customers." A manager happened to be walking by just then and heard the conversation. She stopped and asked the server, "Why don't you tell him the rest of the story?"

To which Jim chimed in, "Yes, why don't you?"

"Well," she replied, "I *earned* my stars by passing written and performance tests. I *keep* my stars by maintaining a certain level of customer satisfaction."

How interesting! Earning stars is accompanied by a certain pay increase. Also, if Jim's server's customer-satisfaction scores fall below a certain level for a particular amount of time, she will not only lose her star but also her *pay rate*. Whether you agree with this method or not, Cracker Barrel does understand that there is often a *big gap* between Levels 2 and 3. They know that sometimes extraordinary steps are required to close that gap, to create sustained positive behaviors, and thus to bring about positive results for the employees, company, and customers.

> **Business Partnership Tip:** Conduct research to find out how well your area or organization is linking Levels 2 (learning) and 3 (on-the-job application) behaviors.

Action-Based Learning as a Driver

Deana Gill has used Action-Based Learning both at Pricewater-houseCoopers and at the Ministry for Children and Family Development on Vancouver Island. Both organizations have determined that this single reinforcing driver is the key to executing some of their key strategies. The following is a detailed description of what it is and how she implements it.

Action-Based Learning in the Workplace

The underlying belief of Action-Based Learning is that real-life situations provide endless opportunities for us to grow and develop. Action-Based Learning is a dynamic, real-time method of training that brings a group of individuals together to identify the cause of real problems and arrive at possible solutions. It then goes one step further by requiring that those solutions be put into action and the results fed back to the group.

When applied in the workplace, Action-Based Learning offers a highly effective method of group training to develop the required competencies, knowledge, and skills required to excel. The magic is in its simplicity, as people learn to pause, reflect, explore, and gain insight to develop the best path of action; they do this by reviewing a real-life, real-time workplace situation. So real work is getting done and the participants are learning valuable lessons at the same time.

What Does Action-Based Learning Look Like in the Workplace?

Action-Based Learning may look different in each organization and each program. In some situations, groups of individuals come together to focus on specific challenges to problem-solve to the point of resolution or to make recommendations for improvement. Or, it may involve using Action-Based Learning as an extension of a curriculum as a means for group discussion and application of the concepts. Applications of Action-Based Learning may be short term or long term, depending on the context and the overarching objectives of the intervention.

According to Deana Gill, "In our experience with a leadership-development program, co-developed and delivered in partnership with Royal Roads University and the Ministry for Children and Family Development on

Vancouver Island, the focus of the Action-Based Learning groups was on regional organizational strategic priorities. Groups of six people across program areas and levels—from administrative staff to supervisors—teamed up to explore leadership challenges related to organizational priorities. Issues such as employee engagement, quality assurance, communication, and work/life balance were explored by the learners. They developed recommendations for possible solutions and actions to address the issues and effect positive change. In this example, the program duration was six months, with core curriculum related to leadership development. The Action-Based Learning projects focused on real-life organizational challenges as a means of anchoring the learning to the workplace."

What Are the Benefits?

The research and feedback related to Action-Based Learning identify all kinds of great benefits beyond effective training, such as:

- Improved organizational relationships

- Increased employee engagement

- Support of creativity and innovation

- Opportunity for collaboration, knowledge sharing, and relationship building in the era of technologically accelerated and disconnected organizations

Not only does Action-Based Learning provide an interactive and dynamic experience for individual development, it can also address the most critical organizational challenges, such as employee engagement, leadership development, and organizational-culture mindset. Very rarely is there a learning and development tool that promotes all levels of change in one fun package!

Deana continued, "In the MCFD (Ministry for Children and Family Development) Action Leadership Program, I witnessed people become transformed into more confident, connected, and motivated contributors in the organization. By honoring the expertise that people possess and inviting them to share their divergent perspectives, this approach taps into the individual and group potential. It also connects them to the organization at a strategic level."

The Brunei Five Ms

Jim worked with a delightful group of business and training leaders at DST Communications in Brunei. When asked to develop a list of drivers, one small group came up with the Five Ms: Mentoring, Motivating, Money, Monitoring, and Measuring. While this may not be an exhaustive list, they are on the right track!

It is important to note that the principles described here are *critical* and *necessary* for the success of any major initiative. But they may not be enough. There needs to be some level of organizational readiness in key areas for your initiative (and the execution of the KBPM) to have a chance of even getting off the ground. The next chapter addresses these foundational issues.

Wendy's Story

I think many of you reading this book can probably relate to the phenomenon that the older we get, the faster the years go. Even though every year has the same 365 days, it seems that we are in an accelerated state once we hit the age of 30. So, back to the story. I left off the last segment wondering if I could continue at my current company in the cocoon of a secure job, where I could spend as much time as I liked building my own knowledge of training. The cost of such comfort was that I would be part of an organization that I felt really didn't "get" training and business partnership.

Well, the years went by. Six and a half of them, to be precise. I stayed with the company. At what cost? I developed acid reflux and until recently had to take a daily acid-blocker pill. I burned some bridges, to be sure. In trying to be true to myself, yet keep a job that allowed me a comfortable lifestyle, there was a price to pay. I think I pursued every possible avenue to help my company see what I could see in terms of training discipline.

I recommended that the entire department take an in-house instructional design course like the one I had taken on my own. I invited co-workers to attend seminars with me. I got a few of us enrolled in ASTD (American Society for Training and Development). I created a fifty-page business case for how to integrate sales training and development into company recruiting, onboarding, and performance appraisals. I created informal alliances with many of the groups that used our training programs. None of these ideas was well received.

I didn't give up. When crossing the metaphorical bridge wasn't a possibility, I grabbed a life vest and swam. And I *hate* swimming! I reverted to a more grassroots approach. I partnered informally with key managers throughout the company. In many cases this worked; in some, it was disastrous. Where I could, I found people who in general believed in the value of training. I built relationships with them so I could better understand their needs, and therefore design better training in partnership with them.

There were some victories, some of them large. For example, I formed a training advisory council made of the key managers of the training-program participants. Their feedback formed the backbone of the sales and customer service training program that many termed the best and most comprehensive the company had ever seen. I created a job aid of all current promotions and offers that was used by most areas of the company. It received accolades as one of the best time-saving tools that had been developed. The field sales team said it was the first thing they referred to when they had a question (rather than the corporately produced tools that were usually out of date by the time they were printed).

My final major accomplishment was creating the first-ever sales meeting kit. This was a train-the-trainer tool designed to help sales managers efficiently communicate information to their sales teams at decentralized offices around the country. A full 100 percent of them agreed that the tool saved countless hours of preparation time and helped them to better deliver the information. So my years at the company definitely had a positive impact.

There were a lot of waves in otherwise calm waters during this time. Let's just say that managers and executives who are very comfortable don't always appreciate someone coming along and rocking their boats! And I was most definitely a boat-rocker. While the successful initiatives yielded many good results, they also threatened others who had not thought of them first. Or those who said they were "not possible." So the "swim" from the training side to the business side was continually through turbulent water.

In my studies I had read about the Kirkpatrick Four Levels evaluation model and I was also attempting to implement as much of it as I could in my training. For example, I personally reviewed and rewrote the quiz questions that were misleading or grammatically incorrect so the quizzes were "passable" by those who knew the information. I participated in a group that revised the Level 1 evaluation so the questions had more substance, and Level 3 predictive questions were also included. I could not say at that time that I was an expert in evaluation, but I was doing everything I could to incorporate it into my training program.

At the end of 2007 (near the end of my tenure at that company), another very lucky thing happened. And this time I knew right away that it was good luck. I saw that my local ASTD chapter would be hosting a seminar with Jim Kirkpatrick. I quickly verified online that he was related to Don Kirkpatrick, the creator of the Four Levels. When I saw that he was, I signed up and crossed my fingers that a business meeting would not pull me out of town that day.

I had to play quite a shell game with my schedule to keep that day open. Fortunately, I was able to attend. I have to say I was surprised how open and humble Jim was. He even offered to look over a class plan I had just finished developing and provide feedback! I sent it to him right away, and I was still a little bit surprised when he called me to discuss it.

Key Points

- Mastering the targeting of critical behaviors and key drivers is a differentiator between the average trainer and a true strategic business partner.

- Critical behaviors are the few, key behaviors that employees have to consistently perform in order to bring about the targeted outcomes.

- Drivers are processes and systems that reinforce, monitor, encourage, or reward performance of critical behaviors on the job.

- More is not better. Identify a manageable number of critical behaviors and required drivers so as to not overwhelm participants and their managers.

- The degree to which you successfully address critical behaviors and required drivers will directly lead to increased Level 4 impact.

8

Step 5: Identify Necessities for Success

"First they ignore you, then they laugh at you,
then they fight you, then you win."

—Mahatma Gandhi

MANY GREAT TRAINING EFFORTS go for naught because the knowledge, competencies, and skills learned fall on *unfertile ground.* This means that when well-meaning and enthusiastic employees return to their jobs, intending to apply what they have learned, sometimes the culture (or their immediate supervisor) discourages them from doing so. Or, they are not clear on what exactly they are supposed to do. Or, they don't have the skill, knowledge, or inclination to do what they know they are supposed to be doing, and no one is helping them.

There are a variety of reasons otherwise good training fails to yield the critical behaviors that produce the targeted outcomes. Hence, Step 5 in the KBPM anticipates and addresses those problems before execution begins.

What Is a "Necessity"?

This step of the KBPM is about doing what you can to set the proper conditions *prior to* any learning interventions, as a way of increasing the likelihood of overall program success. When Jim was a kid, his dad used to make him go around the yard to pick up sticks before he began mowing the lawn, so that he could mow quickly and without interruption. With Jim's prior help, his dad knew he could mow the entire lawn without encountering a stick that could break the mower. So, this preparatory Step 5 helps ensure that your training goes without a hitch.

The last chapter provided ideas for what needs to happen *after* your major learning initiatives. This chapter is about what needs to happen *before*. Did we get this backwards? We don't think so. The fact is that colleagues have told us it is critical to identify and agree on managing the drivers early on. Once the

Kirkpatrick Business Partnership Steps						
P	A	R	T	N	E	R
Pledge	Address	Refine	Target	**NECESSITIES**	Execute	ROE

critical behaviors and required drivers are determined, you know what issues you need to address before the initiative starts.

This order of things brings us to necessities. *Necessities* are prerequisite items, events, conditions, or communications that will help head off problems before they get the chance to reduce the impact of your initiatives.

> ➤ *Necessities:* Prerequisite items, events, conditions, or communications that help head off problems before they reduce the impact of any initiatives.

Here are some examples of necessities for all initiatives that go beyond Level 2:

- Pre-positioning of employees to meet the expectations for their new critical behaviors and to expect monitoring after the training event

- Giving supervisors with coaching skills clear expectations of what will be required of them to reinforce behaviors of training graduates

Representative examples of necessities that vary by company and program are:

- Software that will be required to support the initiative

- Training and tracking systems

- Implementation of a new training model

- Design of an overall evaluation methodology and specific measurement tools

- A new incentive system that supports and rewards new competencies

- Manuals that detail new procedures

- New reporting channels or organizational structures

- Job descriptions updated to reflect new skills and competencies

You will note that the necessities here have been divided into two categories. The first category is for initiatives that go beyond Level 2; these all *require* that the two necessities be addressed. You can count on the fact that preparing the training participants and their supervisors for critical behaviors and executing the required drivers are keys to the success of your initiative.

The second group of necessities are those that vary depending on the company culture and the specific initiative. Some of these are just a matter of preparation; others are deep cultural matters. These also need to be resolved, but attempting to do so will likely encounter resistance and take a lot of effort to resolve. Therefore, they can be worked on parallel to the interventions themselves.

> **Business Partnership Tip:** Take an honest look at root causes when examining training failures. Statistically, the failures seldom stem from the training events themselves; rather, the problems lie in the application environment after the event.

The First Group: Necessities for All Initiatives

Though we need to talk about both kinds of necessities, let's begin with those that apply to all kinds of training initiatives—for all situations and all types of companies.

Preparing Participants for Training

To understand the importance of preparing the training participants for what they will learn, what they need to do back on the job, and that they will be monitored, here is a story from Tom Trifaux of Calgary, Canada. He was a professional football player for six years in the Canadian Football League, now an HRD professional. He told us that after every game, he had to sit in an assistant coach's office and watch a film of the game— and, specifically, his performance. The coach then "offered a few gentle suggestions as to how he could improve his performance." (That is, he screamed his head off at him!) Here it was: a 6-foot 5-inch, 300-pound football player saying he was more nervous about his coaching session on Monday than he was facing his opponent the day before!

What does this have to do with necessary pre-conditions? In this case, it is telling you that before you implement any kind of Level 3 evaluation methodology—which in a sense involves observing and judging people's performance—you had better set the table first. Let the individuals know *why* you will be doing it (i.e., to help them perform better) and *how* you will go about it. Otherwise, people will freak out.

Prior notification is only fair and appropriate. It is necessary to tell those involved that follow-up will occur, and that the purpose of the program is to help the graduates of this training initiative to apply their new knowledge, not to catch them doing something wrong. It is especially a good idea to point out to the participants during the training that there will be follow-up afterwards (if indeed there will be). Present the news in a spirit of helpfulness—helping the participants succeed, in order to enhance their skill sets, make them more valuable and more promotable, and ultimately bring a positive impact to the customers/patients/clients and the business.

There are two benefits to properly preparing your participants for the behavior execution and monitoring. First, when people know they will be monitored and measured, they are more likely to perform the required behaviors. Second, these became data that will contribute to the Chain of Evidence you are building to present in the final step, ROE.

The Importance of Job Aids

At the risk of stating the obvious, we will say that the best way to make training graduates feel comfortable about being monitored is to provide resources to help them to get the behavior right in the first place! At this step, you can create job aids and think about what reminders and reinforcements are appropriate to encourage those desired behaviors. Job aids are a great way to help both participants and supervisors stay on track. They are great reminders of the training and also serve as guides for the participants' progress through the reinforcement period.

Keep your job aids short—no more than two sides of one page. More is not better here. The simpler and clearer the tool, the more likely it will be used. If you feel that you have more information than can be conveyed on one page, consider using graphics instead of lengthy explanations. Use bulleted lists and highlight key words instead of block paragraphs of full sentences. If your company has a graphics department, consider enlisting an artist to help you effectively communicate your message.

> **Business Partnership Tip:** Consider asking a graphic artist to format your aids, using diagrams, illustrations, and bulleted points to convey key points concisely.

Table 8-1 is an example of a completed job aid from the Region of Waterloo in Ontario, Canada, one of our stars. Participants were given a blank version of this form to fill out at the end of training.

Preparing Supervisors to Perform Required Drivers

Equally important to preparing the training participants is preparing their supervisors to perform the required drivers that will support those new behaviors. Jim learned the hard way many years ago what can happen if you don't take this vital step.

About fifteen years ago, Jim taught a series of Total Quality Management (TQM) courses to a large group of line bank em-

TABLE 8-1. Tools and Tips for Your Training Session

Insights	Tools / Techniques	Things to Try in the Next 2–4 Weeks
• Charlie is an introvert. I need to give him more time to reflect on an issue before asking for his ideas. • I don't do a very good job giving positive and constructive feedback. • The clutter in my office is a stressor.	• Count to 10 after asking, "Are there any questions?" • Spend an equal amount of time clarifying the problem as you do generating solutions. • "Feedback Formula": Describe the behavior; impact on you; impact on others; what to do same or different. • Focus on my sphere of control—focus versus influence. • Spend time each day appreciating the day.	• I am going to use feedback formula to give 5 people positive feedback in the next 2 weeks. • I am going to write my next report to include executive summary so that the "Ns" will be able to more easily comprehend. • I am going to take a lunch break 2–3 times a week. • I am going to stop gossiping at breaks, as it is not helping me with my stress.

ployees. The material was good and relevant. The facilities were conducive to learning. The coffee was hot. And the instructor did a good job. So, Level 1 was covered.

Jim also had observable and measurable evidence that the participants learned what was intended. So, Level 2 was covered. But one of the basic skills that they learned was how to flowchart their key job processes, and here is where the wheels fell off the bus. One of the participants, Mary, came to me a few weeks after her training and said, "Jim, I really enjoyed your class and learned a lot. Unfortunately, when I returned to my desk and started flowcharting one of my processes, my boss happened by. He looked over my shoulder at what I was doing and said in a gruff tone, 'You'll *not* be drawing pictures on my watch.'"

Well, that was not only the end of the TQM line for Mary but also for the entire initiative. Jim had made the fatal error of not preparing the supervisors to understand and support what their employees had learned. And this happens all the time! We have heard similar horror stories from well-meaning professionals who trained large groups of people in topics such as "Handling Difficult Conversations" and "Creativity and Innovation." In both cases, the ground was not prepared, and subsequently the managers were not prepared. In the first instance, they were not open to being "confronted" by their employees; in the second, the company's culture frowned on risk taking. The end result? Lots of time and money wasted, and the unintended reinforcement of a culture of fear and discouragement.

Now is the time to communicate the full scope and purpose of your training initiative to supervisors, in particular highlighting how they will support it. Mike Woodard from Georgia-Pacific, the Strategic Learning Services department from Edward Jones, and others use some sort of a *kick-off meeting*. Mike's was more in the form of a meeting. Edward Jones developed and hosted an internal mini-conference to ensure their training professionals were all synchronized with the forthcoming changes in the role of training within the firm. The Strategic Learning Services department also has a project specific kick-off process which drives the business partnership concept. In both cases, the purpose is to make sure that everyone is clear about the purposes of the initiative, the desired outcomes, the methodology that will be used, timing and milestones, and the specific tasks that every person involved is to perform. Also, the process of how each role will be *monitored and supported* is explained.

We use a tool that helps participants and managers realize the importance of attending to training issues before and after the actual event. We reserve it for mission-critical programs. This is a job aid that explains the entire initiative to supervisors (as well as your jury), making clear to everyone involved what each person's role and responsibilities are during and after the process. It's a key tool for communicating the scope of an initiative to supervisors and other parties involved. Figure 8-1 shows the aid.

Now, Figure 8-2 is an example of a job aid that is used for coaches at SC Johnson to reinforce training.

Other Necessities for Your Initiatives

The second category of necessities—those that vary depending on the situation—also need to be addressed before any training initiative is implemented. These necessities include the systems, culture, and tools that will underpin your training efforts.

Some of these tasks are simply matters of preparation—for example, making sure that a software program is installed. Most, however, get you into the murky area of cultural issues and procedural changes that require high-level support and, possibly,

FIGURE 8-1. SC Johnson Core Course Program

Pre-Training	Timing	Post-Training	Timing
Participants are identified by a. Enrollment form b. Individualized Action Plan c. Discussion with Manager	Quarterly	Administer Post Program Evaluation a. Level 1 b. Level 2 c. Include plans for L3 and L4	Immediately following program
Coaching Guide Developed a. Consider needs of department b. Consider needs of participant	2 months prior to program	Summary of program sent to participant and manager	Immediately following program
Invitation sent to participant a. Includes logistics b. Includes course objectives (L2–L4)	1 month prior to program	Coaching Guide sent to manager	Immediately following program
Notification is sent to manager a. Includes logistics b. Includes support plan c. Includes course objectives	2 weeks prior to program	L3 and L4 evaluation administered to participant, manager, etc. a. Surveys b. Focus groups	1–6 months following program
		Monitoring of drivers and updating dashboard	1–6 months following program

FIGURE 8-2.   SC Johnson Coaching Worksheet
Coaching Guide for (Program Name)

Purpose of Coaching Guide:

To help you, the supervisor, to assist your employee apply the knowledge and skills he/she learned in the above-mentioned program. As you know, training is only as good as the degree to which the principles are applied. And the degree to which that transfer of learning to behavior occurs will positively and directly impact the degree of your targeted business results.

This Coaching Guide outlines the basic objectives of the workshop, offers some suggestions as to how to reinforce the training that your employee has received, and some general coaching tips.

Workshop Objectives:
1.
2.
3.
4.

Suggestions to Reinforce Training
1. Review the objectives to ensure clarity of expectations.
2. Reinforce the behaviors you see him/her doing right.
3. Develop an accountability system (like an action plan) to ensure compliance of mission-critical behaviors.
4. Discuss barriers to effective application.
5. Meet regularly for critical behaviors.
6. Discuss impact so employee can see ultimate purpose.
7. Discuss additional training and development needs.

General Coaching Suggestions
1. Do more listening than talking.
2. Check for clear understanding and agreement of expectations.
3. Be open to identification of barriers and possible solutions.
4. Keep a coaching log.
5. Avoid distractions.
6. Help to remove barriers and facilitate additional development.

formal approval. Address these matters at this step, before the execution of the program, to allow adequate time for those often slow wheels of change in a large company to get moving. Here's an example of what can happen if you don't resolve these important issues, or if you pretend that the facts don't exist.

Facing the Brutal Truth

Wendy talks about the necessity of sometimes facing the brutal truth. In the world of business, this often means also bringing up unpopular topics, such as cultural, behavioral, and interpersonal issues, that are derailing important initiatives. In fact, this will likely be part of the process for you, so be ready.

For example, Wendy had a boss who was in love with big training events. Previously he had hosted many events set up as trade shows, with keynote presentations, breakout sessions, and an expo hall filled with product and program displays. These events were well attended in the 1990s, and even into the early part of the 2000s. However, her boss refused to acknowledge the fact that trade show attendance was dropping as an overall industry trend. Also, he wouldn't admit that people now could obtain information in more efficient ways: on the Internet, via e-learning, and with "lunch and learn" programs that didn't take as much time and or cost as much money. Finally, he didn't see that the company could better invest its limited training funds in these more efficient and effective means of disseminating information and encouraging learning.

Despite all evidence to the contrary, her boss kept pushing for more large events. Some of them did come to fruition, but they were poorly attended and were unprofitable. But most of the proposed events got weeded out during the budgeting process. This only served to make the training department look foolish and unconcerned about the need of the business to make a profit. His clinging to the obsolete "large training event" prevented more innovative and relevant mobilization of the training team in areas like e-learning, coaching, and development of informal learning tools and job aids. This stance compromised the entire department, which consequently experienced a significant budget cut each year. As this book was going to press, Wendy heard that her old boss had been asked to take early retirement, and that what remained of the training group reported to the marketing department.

So, the advice is, face the brutal truth. Realize that changes will impact your initiatives, and you have no choice but to accept those changes before your execution starts. Trying to move forward with the proverbial "elephant in the room" will not work, and will waste a lot of your time and resources. It will also damage your credibility in the eyes of the jury.

The good news is, however, that you show "your jury" that you *can* face the brutal truth about training. In this book, you will encounter many brutal truths about the training business that will impact the success of your initiatives if you do not address them in advance—particularly in Step 5. As we indicated at the beginning of this section of the chapter, there will be sensitive topics that link up to matters of improving employee engagement and morale, as well as business productivity. Wendy particularly recommends finding an executive champion to frame the conversation and provide credibility (particularly if you are not an executive yourself). Especially in an organization steeped in tradition, having an advocate will help you move your initiative forward rather than crush it before it can even be begun.

Kirkpatrick's Business Partnership Quiz

As a means of tackling these cultural issues, we developed the following Business Partnership Quiz. It will help you identify areas of weakness in your organization that may end up being barriers to the successful execution of your training program. Take a couple of minutes to see how you do.

Directions: Review the 15 statements. Each addresses an important component of the formula for successful execution of training—that is, in a way that the bottom line is positively impacted. Objectively respond to each statement, assigning 1 to 3 points depending on the degree to which your department or function corresponds with the statement: 3 = high, 2 = medium, 1 = low.

1. I receive frequent and relevant requests for learning interventions from line business leaders in regard to their business problems, needs, or opportunities.
2. We have a good process by which to determine whether business requests are truly training-related.
3. Our program-development processes are aligned with business needs.
4. When assessing the needs of stakeholders, we negotiate the expectations and identify what success will look like at Levels 3 (Behavior) and 4 (Results).
5. We engage subject matter experts in the design and development of our programs.
6. Prior to training, managers and supervisors share with participants their expectations for the training and subsequent application of those skills on the job.
7. We utilize business leaders in the delivery of key training programs.
8. We establish specific job competencies and weave them into the training.
9. We use evaluation to eliminate snags at Levels 1, 2, and 3 to ensure that the training provides maximum value at Level 4 (Results).

10. We conduct effective impact studies on the training programs to demonstrate the business value of learning.
11. We use Level 3 (Behavior) to determine if knowledge and skills haven't been transferred to the job because of faulty training or problems with the culture of the business unit.
12. We successfully partner with business managers and supervisors, using feedback and their coaching of direct reports to maximize the impact of training.
13. We develop effective job aids for both participants and managers to leverage what is learned in training.
14. We use technology to streamline the training and evaluation.
15. We use effective presentation skills to demonstrate the value of learning to the company's bottom line.

Use the following as your rating scale: 45–40, excellent; 39–33, very good; 32–27, good; 26–21, fair; 20–15, poor.

Business Partnership Tip: Ask trusted business leaders in your organization to take the quiz, then discuss with them what can be done to improve the culture of training.

Samples of Necessities from Our Stars

Our star companies provide a diverse sampling of conditions you are likely to encounter. Table 8-2 shows how they addressed the necessities in each case.

Theses examples are all designed to help determine the necessities for success *prior to* the rollout of any major initiative. Some necessities will take months or longer to build support or to undo past practices. Others are low-hanging fruit that can

TABLE 8-2.   Star Companies and Their Necessities

Company	Necessities
Georgia-Pacific Consumer Products	1. Establish advisory board. 2. Get training staff on board with model. 3. Draft "Learning Contract." 4. Establish methodology and technology for remote coaching. 5. Develop coaching log. 6. Establish peer coaching model. 7. Plan kick-off event.
Edward Jones	1. Review program logistics and revise as necessary. 2. Review communication methods and revise as necessary. 3. Educate all participating training personnel in the process.
Region of Waterloo, Ontario, Canada	1. Prepare Learning Plan guidelines to go out to participants and managers prior to program. 2. Ensure participants complete Myers-Briggs Type indicator for self-awareness purposes. 3. Modify modules based on managers' feedback.
AEGON Canada Inc.	1. Prepare facilitators, participants, and managers to conduct Level 3 evaluation. 2. Prepare Level 3 evaluation tools. 3. Elicit president's commitment to active involvement in program reinforcement. 4. Teach senior leaders how to lead by example.
Ministry for Children and PricewaterhouseCoopers Private Company Services	1. Educate all involved in Action-Based Learning methodology. 2. Clarify roles and responsibilities of stakeholders.

	3. Develop comprehensive evaluation strategy. 4. Plan kick-off event. 5. Pay attention to process as well as task; ongoing communication with facilitators. 6. Establish key performance metrics; track and report on progress.
Allen County Department of Transportation	1. Educate all involved in new approach. 2. Rewrite training materials so they integrate A-DOT's mission and values. 3. Clarify roles and responsibilities. 4. Develop Level 3 and 4 evaluation tools.

easily be instituted and will go a long way toward creating that positive ROE down the road.

One of Mike Woodard's necessities listed in Table 8-2 is to get his training staff at Georgia-Pacific Consumer Products on board with the model. Figure 8-3 is his G-P Corporate University staff meeting agenda for the meeting at which he discussed the nature of the "Managing Remote Team Members" program prior to its rollout.

FIGURE 8-3.   G-P Corporate University Staff Meeting Agenda

Meeting Purpose: A Current Year Update and Look Ahead
Date of Meeting: Monday, June 16, 2008

Desired Outcome	How (Process)	Who	Time
1. An update on the Sales University staff, so everybody is aware of the capabilities moving into the second half of 2008 and into 2009.	Discussion	Mike W	15 min.

(continues)

FIGURE 8-3. (Continued)

Desired Outcome	How (Process)	Who	Time
2. Your feedback of the Training Needs Assessment re-cap binder, so that we can make any adjustments for the 2008 assessment.	Discussion	Group	15 min.
3. Review the 2008 workshops completed to date and the Level 1 evaluation scores, so that we are aligned on this low-level evaluation feedback.	Update & Discussion	Mike W.	30 min.
4. An understanding of our Level 2 assessment (testing) strategy and timeline, so that we are all aligned and set up for success.	Understanding & Confirmation	Group	30 min.
5. An understanding of the "New Hire Orientation" program and release, and how to best prepare hiring managers and yourselves to leverage this powerful tool to its fullest potential.	Update	Group	30 min.
6. An understanding of what scorecarding metrics some corporate universities are using, so that we can formulate our university scorecard with total alignment.	Discussion	Group	45 min.
7. A review of the MVI e-Learning curriculum and your feedback, so that we can share that feedback with MVI.	Discussion	Group	15 min.
8. An understanding of how "pilot" workshops are conducted, so that we are all aligned on expectations and format.	Understanding & Discussion	Group	15 min.
9. A review of the team training schedule for the remainder of this year, so that we are all aligned on the topics and dates.	Discussion	Group	20 min.
10. Review of the University's policies and several attendance issues, so that we are all aligned on each policy and its reason for being.	Review & Discuss	Mike W & Group	15 min.

11. An understanding of each of your 2009 and beyond priorities to the best of your abilities, so that we can continue to align to your needs.	Discussion	Group	30 min.
12. Feedback for the University, so that we can better serve your needs for the remaining part of 2008 and into 2009.	Discussion	Group	15 min.
13. An agreement on next steps, so that we are set up for success, moving into 2008.	Review	Mike W	10 min.
12. Plus/Delta of the meeting	Discussion	Mike W	5 min.

The purpose of this and of many of Mike's other meetings is to make sure that his staff members are clear about the overall direction of the Corporate University and their roles in building the business partnerships, and to make sure that all of their initiatives are aligned with the corporation's mission, vision, values, and directives of the corporation.

Setting up for Training Success

The way that the Region of Waterloo, Ontario, handled the necessities for its training initiative was to create letters to both inform the training participants and give notice to the supervisors about their role in the process. Figure 8-4 is the letter sent to employees; Figure 8-5 is the letter sent to the supervisors.

A Detailed Look at the Necessities for Success

We wrap up this chapter by looking at the three approaches to a generational learning program, as introduced in Chapter 5,

FIGURE 8-4. Region of Waterloo Letter to Employees

Dear Employee:

Congratulations on your acceptance into our 3-day Learning to Lead Program on [insert date]. Please consider the criteria below for attendance at this program. You will be asked to:

- Evaluate your leadership qualities and develop a learning plan that you will discuss with your supervisor;
- Practice giving and receiving feedback; and
- Look for opportunities to apply the skills you acquire through the program once you get back to work.

We will be asking your supervisor to support you in your leadership development by discussing your learning objectives and providing you with opportunities to apply the new skills back in the workplace. Below is a template to assist you with these discussions:

Pre-Workshop	Post-Workshop
• Discuss ideas about learning goals and program requirements to determine suitability • Set up a post-workshop meeting time to discuss refined goals and plan of action	• Get feedback on your development goals • Discuss learning plan, action items, and further developmental opportunities • Discuss opportunities for application of new skills and outline the action plan around it, with dates • Be clear about what support you need from your supervisor in order to make this successful

FIGURE 8-5.   City of Waterloo Letter to Supervisors

Dear Supervisor:

Your employee, [insert name], has been accepted to attend the 3-day Learning to Lead Program at the Region on [insert date]. This leadership program is built on three of the Region's Core Leadership Characteristics:

- Self-awareness
- Motivating and developing others
- Managing change

Participants in the Learning to Lead Program will be asked to:

- Develop a learning plan;
- Practice giving and receiving feedback; and
- Look for opportunities to apply the skills he/she acquires through the program.

We are asking you to support [insert name] in her or his leadership development by scheduling time before and after this program to discuss the individual's learning goals and how you can facilitate opportunities for that person to apply those skills back in the workplace. Below is a template to assist you in these discussions:

Pre-Workshop	Post-Workshop
• Discuss ideas about learning goals and program requirements to determine suitability • Set up a post-workshop meeting time to discuss refined goals and plan of action	• Give feedback on employee's development goals • Discuss learning plan and further developmental opportunities • Create opportunities for application of new skills; discuss action plan and dates • Ask what support employee needs from you to make this work

and what some key necessities for success might look like for companies A, B, and C. Table 8-3 shows these three approaches.

Note the words *preparation, development,* and *determine* in the Necessities column. These words capture the essence of this step. Once the necessities have been addressed and issues are resolved (or on their way to resolution), you are ready to move to Step 6, the next chapter.

Key Points

- Necessities are prerequisite items, events, conditions, or communications that help to head off problems before they can reduce the impact of your training initiatives.

- Pre-positioning both the participants and their managers prior to training events is a necessity for almost every type of initiative.

- Other kinds of necessities may involve simple processes, or may involve deep cultural issues that can be difficult to address.

- The degree to which your necessities are dealt with will directly influence the future success of your initiatives.

TABLE 8-3. Necessities for Three Generational Learning Programs

Company	Targeted Outcomes	Critical Behaviors	Required Drivers	Necessities
A	1. 95% attendance of invited employees 2. 4.5 or above on key Level 1 indicators 3. 90% of participants pass posttest	None required	None required	1. Effective training tracking system. 2. Development of Level 1 and Level 2 tools.
B	1. Delivery of a program for managers to detail generational differences and see implications. 2. Relevant generational learning methods woven into major ongoing programs.	1. Effective program development 2. Effective program delivery	1. Monitor and coach development of programs. 2. Monitor and coach delivery of programs	1. Effective training tracking system. 2. Development of Level 1, Level 2, and Level 3 tools. 3. Preparation of development monitors and delivery coaches.
C	1. Improved employee engagement scores across the generations. 2. Improved retention of top talent across the generations.	1. Both of the above. 2. Follow-up data with action steps to raise substandard metrics.	1. Both of the above. 2. Monitor numbers and, if indicated, conduct root-cause analyses for substandard numbers on employee engagement. 3. Monitor actions and coach participants to raise key engagement and retention numbers.	1. Effective training tracking system. 2. Development of Level 1, Level 2, Level 3, and Level 4 tools. 3. Preparation of development monitors and delivery coaches. 3. Determine follow-up actions to raise key engagement and retention numbers. 4. Determine follow-up roles and responsibilities.

9

Step 6: Execute the Initiative

"You can't control the wind, but you can always adjust your sails."
—ANONYMOUS

AS WE MOVE ON to the next step in the Kirkpatrick Business Partnership Model (KBPM), we come to the subject of *execution*—not of a person but of a plan or initiative, although if you don't perform this step well, the results may be your true execution (metaphorically speaking, of course).

Strategic Execution

Jim learned about balanced scorecards at the Harvard School of Business in the late 1990s and early 2000s. At the time, his organization, First Indiana Bank, was moving from a corporation driven by tradition and the budget process to one driven by

Kirkpatrick Business Partnership Steps						
P	A	R	T	N	E	R
Pledge	Address	Refine	Target	Necessities	**EXECUTE**	ROE

strategy. And as the founder and director of their corporate university, Jim was assigned to figure out just how to make that transition. Kaplan and Norton's books *The Balanced Scorecard* and *The Strategy-Focused Organization* were the major sources of the methodology as they successfully moved from an organization of transaction specialists to one of trusted advisors. These books, and the Kaplan/Norton methodology of strategy maps, dashboards, and scorecards, put forth the premise that developing a corporate strategy was easier than executing one.

This insight highlights the first point you need to know about execution in the training context: It involves much more than putting together a training program. Good execution of your initiative also includes reinforcement of critical behaviors and evaluation at all levels of the initiative.

> ▸ *Execution*: The design, development, and delivery of the training program, followed by reinforcement and monitoring of critical behaviors, required drivers, and Level 4 metrics.

Up to this point, we have talked about the need for the KBPM and how to successfully set up an initiative so it achieves targeted business outcomes. Now, we need to look at actually executing the model and putting the information you gathered into practice.

The Essential Components

Here are the elements that make up Step 6 of the model:

- Determine the required KSAs (knowledge, skills, attitudes), or learning objectives

- Consider the necessary learning environment

- Design and build the learning program and evaluation tools

- Deliver the program

- Measure Level 1 (Reaction) and Level 2 (Learning)

- Initiate ongoing reinforcement and monitoring

- Measure Level 3 (Behavior) and Level 4 (Results)

- Analyze and report the findings all along the way, and adjust and repeat steps as necessary

Business Partnership Tip: The execution phase doesn't end when the last training class is over. Execution includes reinforcing and monitoring the critical behaviors, ensuring that the required drivers are being used, and reporting the findings to the jury on a regular basis.

Business Partnership Tip: The beginning of the execution step is a good time to confirm that the scope of the initiative has not crept into another realm or grown too large to manage—or shrunken to the point that the desired outcomes will not be realized.

Determine the Required Learning Objectives

The first consideration to address in the execution step is the creation of learning objectives for the training program. This means thinking about the KSAs (knowledge, skills, and attitudes) or competencies that are needed for participants to be able to perform the critical behaviors identified in Step 4. The process should be brief and straightforward, since these behaviors and the required drivers have already been defined.

The key to developing good learning objectives is to make sure that they clearly, directly, and linearly point to the critical behaviors you have identified as necessary to yield desired outcomes. Include nothing more and nothing less.

Consider the Necessary Learning Environment

We address the necessary learning environment (Level 1) at this point. By *environment* we mean the venue and modality for training. Keeping your learning objectives and critical behaviors in mind, think about what type of training will leave participants ready and willing to perform those behaviors.

This is where your traditional training expertise comes into play. Remember Wendy's story about giving a lecture to store associates to "teach" them how to use a cutting apparatus to properly size the wire closet shelving? If one of your key behaviors is a physical process that the participants will have to perform, you need to convince your jury that nothing less than a skills demonstration and hands-on training will suffice.

It's appropriate to jump ahead here a bit and also talk about environment in terms of Level 1 (Reaction) measurement. Traditionally, a "smile" sheet measures Level 1; participants are asked about somewhat related things like the catering, room temperature, and how much they enjoyed listening to the instructor. Take your training to a higher level and consider what reactions or environmental considerations contribute to effective learning of critical behaviors. Focus your attention on (and include on the evaluation form) those things, too.

Design and Build the Learning Program and Evaluation Tools

From there, we move to the design and development of the learning program. Since most learning professionals currently spend the bulk of their time in the "design and deliver" mode, we need not spend a lot of time explaining how to translate learning objectives into course materials. Here's just one reminder: make sure you fully explain the purpose of the critical behaviors in terms of their contribution to key business outcomes. And explain exactly how those behaviors will be monitored, reinforced, encouraged, rewarded, or whatever else you plan to do during execution. All participants should complete the training with a clear understanding of what they will be expected to do on the job.

We would also like to remind you to keep scope creep in mind. At Wendy's last company, one thing they did well was consider what information should be included in their training programs and, just as important, what shouldn't be included. They categorized all of the possible content as "need to know" and "nice to know." The "need to know" items were necessary to bring the learning objectives to life. The "nice to know" items were either included in an appendix (so the facilitator knew how to field questions) or left out. Especially during down times in the economy, stick to the "need to know" during your training program! If something doesn't relate to helping a participant know how and why to perform the critical behaviors, it doesn't need to be included.

Importantly (and often forgotten) at this point, you also need to determine the best way to measure each of the four levels, and to build the tools and measurement plan you will use. This helps you create measurement tools with substance—ones that measure the things that really count. There will be no more slapping together a "smile sheet" at the last minute and calling it evaluation!

Table 9-1 is a list of common methods and tools that are useful in measuring each of the four levels. Please refer to our other books to learn how to implement these methods.

TABLE 9-1. Means for Evaluation

| Methods | Evaluation Levels | | | |
	1 Reaction	2 Learning	3 Behavior	4 Results
Survey	●	●	●	●
Questionnaire/interview	●	●	●	●
Focus group	●	●	●	●
Knowledge test/check		●		
Skills observation		●	●	
Presentation		●		
Action planning and monitoring		●	●	●
Action-Based Learning			●	
Key business HR metrics				●

Deliver the Program and Measure Levels 1 and 2

In whatever modality and venue you selected earlier, now is when you deliver the program. Again, we believe most training professionals are experienced in delivering training programs, so we will not add a lot of detail here. Just don't forget to tell participants exactly how they will be monitored, coached, and rewarded on the job for performing the behaviors you have taught them.

This is also when formal evaluating begins, with Levels 1 and 2. Once you have the Level 1 and Level 2 data, take the time to analyze it and check for possible problems. If you have concerns about reactions to the training or whether the participants are learning, schedule a meeting with your jury members to discuss quick remediation options. Don't wait until the end of the initiative to analyze and share data that may indicate the need to loop back and rework a step.

In the likely event that Level 1 and Level 2 data reflect that participants have learned the critical behaviors, share those findings with your jury and also save the information for inclusion in your Chain of Evidence that you will present in Step 7, ROE.

Initiate Ongoing Reinforcement and Monitoring

The execution step moves into new territory for many learning professionals, as you turn your attention to ongoing reinforcement and monitoring. This is when training graduates are performing the critical behaviors, with the support and monitoring by the required drivers.

Once the kick-off or rollout for initiatives has occurred, begin monitoring and coaching the key processes *immediately*, to ensure that there is no initial confusion and that everyone gets off to a good start. It is also important that all involved quickly see that this is not a flavor-of-the-month initiative and that if they wait it will simply run its course, whether everyone complies or not. This initiative has to start strong and stay the course.

This is also the time to partner with the managers and supervisors who are responsible for ongoing coaching and reinforcement. While they will be taking the lead in most cases, you have a strong supporting role as well. Offer any assistance you can and follow up frequently. It is of upmost importance that you, as a learning professional, make it as easy as possible for your training graduates to perform the critical behaviors on the job. It's equally important that you help your business partners to reinforce those behaviors by regularly using the required drivers.

While this step looks like one small bit, it actually can represent months or even years of effort for large initiatives. Now is when you see 50 percent of learning effectiveness occur. It's when you can prevent 70 percent of the potential learning failures, as well. Remember: Execution is *not* complete when the training class is over!

> **Business Partnership Tip:** While initiating the ongoing reinforcement and monitoring sounds like one small step in the Kirkpatrick model, it is critical to achieving a successful outcome for your initiative.

Measure Level 3 and Level 4

Part of your plan will include a timeline for when you will make the "official" measurements of Level 3 (Behavior) and Level 4

(Results). It is fairly obvious that it takes time for most behaviors to be implemented and become part of a graduate's everyday routine. So while you will be monitoring the critical behaviors all along, you may want to wait a few months before making your key measurements. The exact time period you choose depends on how important and how complicated the critical behaviors are.

To illustrate this point, let us give an example. Jim was traveling by air the day after a security breach at London's Heathrow airport in 2005, which resulted in the introduction of the current liquid, gel, and aerosol security restrictions that are still in place. In the security lines at the airport, the TSA supervisors were watching over the shoulders of the associates who were monitoring the X-ray tunnel. A supervisor picked up Jim's suitcase as it emerged from the tunnel, and said the dreaded phrase, "Sir, is this bag yours?" If you travel a lot, you know what this means: Either you have mistakenly left a liquid item in your bag, have been selected for additional screening (and delays), or have otherwise broken a rule and will be detained a while. Jim confirmed that the bag was his, and the supervisor asked to open it; when he did, he pulled out a can of shaving cream. He turned around and showed it to the TSA associate who was monitoring the X-ray machine and said, "This is exactly what we are looking for."

The interval you wait before measuring and monitoring critical behaviors depends on the nature of the behavior and the circumstances. In this case, the security of everyone traveling by air was at risk, so the behavior was monitored and measured right away. Conversely, if the critical behavior for your initiative is the accurate completion of business plans, then you may have to wait until there is a business plan to be completed.

Analyze and Report Findings Along the Way, and Adjust and Repeat Steps as Necessary

Trainers must measure and present their data to the jury during the running of their major initiatives. Don't wait until the end, when it is time for the final report and then present it all at once. Space out your reports. There are four major reasons for this.

First, you need to be monitoring the adoption of those critical behaviors, use of the required drivers, and the preliminary Level 4 outcomes to make sure that things are on track. This is your early warning detection system. If and when critical behaviors aren't being adopted, or required drivers indicate standards are falling, you need to conduct a quick analysis to see what is causing the dip, and as quickly as possible intervene to get the initiative back on track.

Second, you need to pass that information along to your stakeholders (your jury members) to reassure them that you are on track. Third, if your metrics indicate a fall below standard, and you do not have authority or power to remedy the situation, you may need to elicit the help of certain jury members—most likely, the official sponsor of the program or other members of the business partnership team.

Finally, this data will eventually make up significant input into your Chain of Evidence.

To summarize, here are the benefits of performing evaluation during the execution process:

1. If results are not on track, you have time to make adjustments.
2. Early findings offer reassurance to the jury that the program is on track.
3. You have evidence to provide to higher-level managers if you need their support to go beyond your authority or the scope of the program.

4. You are collecting valuable evidence.

As gathering the data is much like the discovery process in the legal profession, let's have another definition.

> ▸ *Discovery:* Procedures by which you gather evaluation data and other information for your programs, processes, and other initiatives.

Indeed, this information gathering is akin to the trial attorney's presenting bits and pieces to the jury as the trial moves along. My attorney friends point out that during the trial, the objective and subjective evidence is often fragmented and (seemingly) disconnected. It is only at the end—during closing arguments—that all the pieces are brought together.

The Presentation of Evidence

Dashboards and scorecards are excellent tools for presenting your data along the way. The dashboard in Figure 9-1 is an example of the way your business partners would probably appreciate seeing data on a monthly basis.

You may be wondering at this point exactly how you will gather the data to populate such a scorecard if hard numbers are not something your initiative is likely to yield. Not every initiative can be quantified so specifically, and that's okay if you and your jury agreed to softer targeted outcomes. For example, Mike Woodard at Georgia-Pacific Consumer Products believes that many professionals make the Level 4 work harder than it needs to be following the dashboard is an example of an e-mail he sometimes sends to senior managers of training participants to gather more subjective data in lieu of or in addition to hard data.

FIGURE 9-1. Dashboard to Show Training Results

Example: Valdez University
Strategic Goal Scorecard—Goal #1

⇑ Up from last month

⇓ Down from last month

⇔ Same as last month

Help to move our organization from transaction-oriented to "trusted advisor"

Metric	Actual	Target	Status
1. Level 1 satisfaction scores—aggregate	93%	90%	⇑
2. % courses learning objectives matched to new directive	85%	70%	⇑
3. Level 2 skills scores—aggregate	92%	90%	⇔
4. % leaders certified as trusted advisor coaches	66%	65%	⇔
5. Level 3 scores—aggregate	48%	75%	▮
6. Gallup scores—aggregate	77%	90%	⇓

Key:

▬ = above target

▬ = on target

▬ = somewhat below target

▬ = significantly below target

Georgia-Pacific Consumer Products Best Practice #3

Dear Colleague,

Your team of professional salespeople recently completed a sales skills development program entitled "Sales Excellence for Large Accounts" about nine months ago. We in the University are interested in determining the business impact of that skill development. Please take a few minutes to answer the following critical questions to help us gauge the impact of the investment of time and money.

1. Have you seen any change in key sales results over the past nine months? If so, please provide specific details.

2. Are you able to attribute any of that change to the sales skill development and subsequent follow-up that your people went through? If so, do you have any evidence to support your conclusion? Please provide.

3. What, if any, feedback have you seen or heard from the customers since your team members attended the skill development?

Thank you for your time.

Best Regards,

[Signature]

The soft evidence gathered in this manner is often extremely credible with jury members. They might say, "If the senior business leaders of the people going through training find it of benefit, and have evidence to show it, it's good enough for us!"

The data and soft evidence that Mike gathers from this simple method is akin to the legal term *affidavit*.

▸ *Affidavit*: A written, printed, or videotaped declaration or statement of facts, made voluntarily and confirmed by the good name of the party making it.

Fiona Betivoiu, from AEGON Canada Inc., provides another example of how she conducted her Level 3 evaluation for the "Leading Edge" leadership program. Here are her comments.

AEGON Canada Inc. Best Practice #2

"During this five-month program in 2008, thirty-six participants took part in a series of training modules, amounting to about sixty hours of training. Training modules included 'Excellence in Leadership,' 'Time Management,' 'Behavioral Interviewing,' 'Conflict Management,' a $2^{1}/_{2}$-day coaching program, and others. In total, there were twelve training modules.

"Four months after the participants graduated, I met individually with each graduate and conducted a Level 3 evaluation. This occurred after I had met with Jim Kirkpatrick in Toronto. In fact, I had not done interviews before. I was trying to get motivated and really see the need to conduct so many of them! Jim suggested that I not meet with everyone, but consider doing an online assessment. In the end, I didn't take that advice. After meeting with a few people individually, I discovered that the Level 3 gave me so much insight and offered a coaching opportunity. Graduates were open about their changes in behavior, and also gave me feedback about the program itself.

"A co-worker named Brittany Major created the interview questions covering each of the core objectives from the training sessions. They were all open-ended, behavioral-interview type questions with an accompanying rating sheet. Here's an example of a question used to determine the effectiveness of our coaching module: 'Please describe a time you have consciously tailored either your behavior or your coaching of someone from one of the four personality styles.' From their answers, it was very easy to tell if they recalled what the personality styles were, and if they could give examples of how and when their behavior changed.

"In addition to these questions, I observed graduates at their work space and reviewed how they had set up their desks, organized their Microsoft Outlook view, and how many e-mails they had, etc. This observation was a 'surprise' for them, and there were core documented things I was looking for. Since one of the training modules taught them how to reorganize their Microsoft Outlook settings and better manage their day, I wanted to check to see if four months later this was actually working! We had amazing success here, by the way—about 80 percent of the group had made great changes to how they were organizing their day and managing their e-mails."

So you're not off the hook in terms of ongoing evaluation and reporting, even if your initiative lacks the hard numbers to report. Whatever the targeted outcomes, critical behaviors, and required drivers you identified, they need to be monitored closely and frequently throughout the initiative, then reported on a regular basis to your jury. This is an important building block in your transformation from learning deliverer to strategic business partner in the eyes of your stakeholders.

Now comes the fun part! In Step 7, you put together your Chain of Evidence and present your Return on Expectation story to the jury.

Key Points

- The execution step includes program design, development, delivery, and extensive reinforcement and reporting. It is much more than just the delivery of a training class.

- Make sure to weave your evaluation strategy into the program design.

- Facilitate, monitor, and report on participants' critical behaviors and the required drivers throughout the course of the initiative.

- Regular measuring and reporting of Levels 3 and 4 evaluation results gives you and the jury the data to determine if adjustments are required during execution to ensure that targeted outcomes are accomplished.

10

Step 7: ROE^{SM}, or Return on Expectations^{SM}

"Try not to become a man of success,
but rather try to become a man of value."
—ALBERT EINSTEIN

YOU HAVE ALL SEEN television news cameras focus on the faces of defendants in highly publicized trials as they hear the words from the judge to the jury foreman: "Have you reached a verdict? And how do you find the defendant?" And then the response either "guilty" or "not guilty" is heard in criminal trials, or "We find in favor of . . ." in civil trials. Remember the look on the defendant or plaintiff's face? It is usually either great joy or great shock and sorrow, depending on the verdict.

This chapter is about hearing the verdict you want and have worked so hard to hear. But first, let's look at the Kirkpatrick Business Partnership steps.

Kirkpatrick Business Partnership Steps						
P	A	R	T	N	E	R
Pledge	Address	Refine	Target	Necessities	Execute	ROE

The Culmination of Hard Work

Jim owned a home not too many years ago near Indianapolis, Indiana. He especially loved the back yard—some trees, flowers, a barn to keep my fishing equipment in, a fire pit, a nice lawn, and . . . an ugly area of gravel. This gravel area was about 20 foot square and had been carefully laid down by the previous owners, for reasons unknown. Jim put up with it for about a year, then decided to get rid of it and replace it with beautiful, lush grass. Little did he know what he was in for. First, Jim had to get rid of the gravel. For the next two weeks, he shoveled it into a wheelbarrow, loaded it onto a tarp in the back of his small SUV, and drove it to a dump site.

To Jim's dismay, he then found a layer of smaller gravel under the larger gravel layer he had just removed. So, another week of backbreaking work to get rid of that gravel, too. Next was a layer of nasty sand that he shoveled and hauled away. Finally, he got down to the dirt. Jim then rented a roto-tiller to break up the ground, added some topsoil, set up his scarecrow, spread fertilizer, and sprinkled on the grass seed. After putting down some straw to "keep the birds away," he began a regimen of watering. Day and night, he kept the soil and those precious

Blend Objective and Subjective Evidence

Notice that we have referred to the evidence as data *and* information. In most trials, and in most of life, being able to convince someone of something requires varied pieces of evidence—and more, if your case is hard to prove. This advice flies in the face of any thinking that a single bit of evidence (e.g., cost/benefit numbers or percentages) is going to convince a corporate jury. As in any trial, your jury is made up of different types of people, with different personalities and preferences. You need to try to address them all. (By the way, this runs parallel with current adult learning theory that says blended learning is better than any single modality.)

Here, it pays big dividends to know your jury and what type of evidence is going to be most compelling for them. In real trials, there are basically two types of evidence—that supplied by expert witnesses and that supplied through testimonies of people affected by the event, often referred to as the "weeping widow." Table 10-1 provides some insights into the differences between the two.

Business guru Tom Peters talked about needing to "capture the hearts and minds of customers." The same is true here. You need to capture the hearts of your jury members through testimonies and capture their minds through data from expert witnesses.

Tell the Story of Success

You will have the best chance of convincing your jury of the significant contribution you have made if you tell a story. That story might include pictures, metaphors, data, and your Level 4

TABLE 10-1. Types of Evidence

Type of Witness	Courtroom Evidence	Business Partnership Evidence	Type of Person Who Relates Best
Expert Witness	Charts, graphs, cause-and-effect relationships, measurements, time frames, relevant documents	Charts, graphs, survey results, test scores, simulation and on-the-job checklists, sales and ops numbers, retention	People who need to see the facts; left-brain oriented
Weeping Widow	Testimonies of people affected by the actions of others	Testimonies of people affected by business partnership initiatives	People who are drawn by stories of changed lives; right-brain oriented

evidence, presented in a way that they can see the story of your success.

Provide Evidence When Proof Is Not Possible

It is time to remind you of another courtroom term, *preponderance of evidence.*

> ► *Preponderance of evidence:* The greater weight of evidence, or evidence that is more credible and convincing to the mind and the heart.

Our stand on demonstrating value is, and has always been, to provide evidence when proof is not possible. In the case of civil trials, attorneys need only provide a preponderance of evidence, not proof beyond a reasonable doubt, as in criminal trials.

Showcase Your Prime Examples

Keep in mind that, in most cases, you get only *one good shot* to convince the jury that: (1) not only was your application of the business partnership model successful in providing value to the organization, but that (2) future efforts will likely yield the same results. This is *not* a "once and done" impact study. Rather, it is your best opportunity to get support, funding, resources, and sponsorship for similar efforts in the future. Make sure that you showcase *your* key witnesses and best evidence.

Save Your Best Presentations for Your Big Cases

The scenario we present here should be reserved for your initiatives in which much is at stake. For programs and initiatives of lesser importance or with lesser impact, settle out of court. In other words, pass along the evidence, but save your best work for face-to-face contacts with your juries.

A Last Look at Some of Our Stars

Let's have a final look at some of our case studies. Notice that all along we have been presenting both data *and* testimony—that is, both objective and subjective evidence. We hope that you are almost convinced of the value of this approach.

Farm Credit Canada

Farm Credit Canada (FCC) achieved some remarkable results as they partnered their way to a culture of 100% accountability, with a series of training and reinforcement initiatives being launched in 2003 and continuing through 2006. The employee engagement scores were as follows: 2002, 68%; 2003, 69%; 2004, 81%; 2005, 84%; 2006, 82%; 2007, 83%; 2008, 81%.

Here's what a couple of employees had to say about the training:

> "I believe this is one of the best initiatives I have seen at FCC and in my prior career as well. The cultural changes have allowed more open dialogue and a safe environment for everyone."

> "I have grown as an individual as a result of culture transformation and there is nothing I can do that would ever repay FCC for that experience and growth."

In terms of business success, since 2002:

- The portfolio almost doubled, from $7.7 billion to over $13 billion.

- There were record levels of new lending and profitability every year, in spite of challenges in agriculture.

- There was growth in market share relative to Canadian banks.

FCC used this data and other information—evidence—to make a compelling presentation to key stakeholders.

Region of Waterloo, Ontario, Canada

Next, we visit the Region of Waterloo. One thing that the OD consultants pointed out to us was that their evidence stopped at Level 3. They did not take the significant change in leadership behaviors to the final level—Level 4. Instead, they linked their program to their Seven Core Leadership Characteristics. Fortunately, their efforts were embraced as being significant. The leadership team from the Region of Waterloo *did* recognize the evidence that the occurrence of targeted, new behaviors will, in all probability, lead to targeted results.

Their next pass at this program will be to identify success indicators and link their efforts and their evidence to that end.

Georgia-Pacific Consumer Products

Mike Woodard is a big proponent of and expert in Action-Based Learning. He especially likes to use it when his sales or operations people are involved with programs that emphasize innovation and creativity. Typically, his Action-Based Learning follow-up consists of small groups of graduates being assigned a task such as rolling out new products to a new market. Graduates develop a plan for that rollout using the knowledge and skills they learned in their training.

After twelve to sixteen weeks, each team of graduates sits in front of a team of high-level, decision-making executives, who judge which plan is the best and award an internal contract to that team. In other words, the jury finds in favor of one team, and rewards it accordingly.

Clarian Health

Linda Hainlen and her Clarian learning/business team worked hard to encourage employees to use the new medication charting and scanning software that was designed to increase compliance, safety, and satisfaction for patients. Below is a review of the background and some of the data she used to make her case.

• *Background:* "One of our most recent implementations was medication charting and scanning software. We trained the masses and as usual, could prove the attendees had gained knowledge. However, when we ran reports, we found that not everyone was using the newfound knowledge. Now, that doesn't mean they weren't charting. They just weren't charting the way we had instructed them, which would allow us to truly improve patient safety and utilize the system for knowledge-driven care."

• *Action Plan:* "We teamed with the managers and put a plan in place. First, we completed a Level 3 evaluation with 90 percent of the staff who had attended training. After the evaluation, our instructional staff provided remediation to fill knowledge gaps. At the same time management reviewed the reports and reiterated the importance of complying with the new method. Then we ran the same reports again."

• *Results:* "Compliance had gone up 33 percent!"

According to Linda, "The reports became the Level 4 validation that management wanted. We exceeded their expectations! The reports also showed the managers who needed continued 'encouragement.' The key was twofold: We included the managers in the solution, and we worked toward performance, not just knowledge. The Kirkpatrick Four Levels have truly helped us impact our organization. I now have evidence of our value that management can understand." Table 10-2 summarizes Linda's results with the program.

TABLE 10-2.   Clarian Health Results on Software Training Program

Unit	Post-Implementation (% of Compliance)	Post–Level 3 (% of Compliance)	Increase (%)
1	80.97	93.85	16
2	79.39	92.13	16
3	78.18	95.86	23
4	73.41	81.51	11
5	58.59	88.64	51
6	69.64	97.53	40
7	68.29	92.83	36
8	82.46	99.15	20
9	52.63	97.71	86
Average increase			33

Edward Jones

The huge team that worked, and continues to work, on the "New Financial Advisor Training" initiative had selected a group of measures to create its chain of evidence. Among these measures were:

- Individual performance

- ATL performance

- Daily and weekly reporting from the classes (Level 1 evaluations)

- Field trainer experience and feedback

- Data from exit interviews

- Series 7 pass rate

- Series 66 pass rate

- Trainee attrition

- Profitability development program metrics

- Percentage of class members who placed an order

Of course, these measures are sequenced so they connect the dots from the program and reinforcement through Level 3 and, ultimately, to Level 4 outcomes.

Stars That Followed the Complete Model

We present two final case studies that, in distinct ways, show the complete chain of evidence that offers what we consider to be fine examples of the Kirkpatrick Business Partnership Model.

Comcast Cable

You will likely not find a case study presented like this anywhere else but here, in this book. Jim Hashman and his team put this together not only to show how to present a compelling Chain of Evidence to a group of business stakeholders but also to creatively weave our courtroom metaphor into the example. The following demonstration and case study data are compliments of Comcast University, under the leadership of Martha Soehren, Ph.D., Comcast's Chief Learning Officer. Jim Hashman, Director of Sales and Retention Learning and Development, at Comcast University, in Philadelphia, Pennsylvania, created the training program and courtroom analogy. The case study data are from an actual Comcast initiative at the St. Paul, Minnesota, call center. There were over three hundred learners involved and nearly thirty members of a supportive management team.

Comcast Cable Call Center Training Initiative

Imagine, if you will, a courtroom complete with jury, judge, prosecutor, bailiff, and court recorder. You, as a training leader, are standing at the defendant's table. The jury is not a group of your peers but, rather, internal clients. The judge is not an appointed pillar of the community but, rather, your company's CEO. The prosecutor is not a lawyer but, rather, much worse: your chief financial officer! Nervous?

- The charge (the worst possible charge that could be leveled against a training leader): Providing training with no evidence of value to the business.

- The penalty, if you are found guilty: A reduction in training resources.

What do you do? Panic? Quit? Cop a plea and offer up your worst trainer? No! You take a deep breath, let out a big sigh, and think to yourself: *Is that all?* You're not worried. Why? Because you have been building a chain of evidence. This chain, via a preponderance of evidence, not only demonstrates that your training creates learning but that it also provides true value to the business by driving positive results!

So where do you start your defense? At the beginning, before the alleged training crime, in the analysis phase. During the needs assessment, you met with your stakeholder and together you determined what was causing their pain. Specifically, the problem was with the metrics being used. Then, once you determined the specific metrics causing the pain, you and your stakeholder determined, and agreed upon, the workplace behaviors that resulted in the targeted business metrics. But you didn't stop there. You continued your needs assessment by establishing both the knowledge and the skills required to demonstrate those targeted behaviors. Finally, you went back to your office and said, "Okay, what experiences and learning methods best fit the knowledge and skill requirements to meet the target behaviors, which will in turn result in the desired business metrics?" Simple, right?

The result of your analysis was a list of goals and expectations. Comcast University wanted to:

- Establish a sales culture (this is not a metric, but was an expectation of training).

- Improve core sales skills (skills that can be observed and therefore can be measured).

- Increase coaching effectiveness (measured by improvement over time; given that the key variable, post-training, is the supervisors' coaching of the targeted skills, trending the performance over time will demonstrate coaching effectiveness).

- Increase revenue (the easiest measure, with several financial metrics available).

- Improve customer satisfaction (customer surveys as the data source).

- Have fun (participation and Level 1 surveys provide insight into learners' experience).

Note: This is an example of beginning with the end result in mind.

The next step in your defense strategy against the heinous charges is to demonstrate training's value by moving from Level 2 to Level 3. This is a change in focus for you—you have mentally moved yourself out of the classroom and into the workplace. You look at your list of goals and expectations to find items that bridge the gap and you hound your client for the data! You also create follow-up activities for on-the-job reinforcement.

At this point, you have conducted the "suspect" training and have collected your Level 1 data; your Level 2 confirmation of learning information; your Level 3 workplace behavior data, validating the desired change; and the targeted business metrics that were causing your client pain. You now have enough data to create a preponderance of evidence. All you need to do is to put it in a logical sequence, and you're ready to mount your defense.

The last step, in this court of training effectiveness, is to mount your defense by presenting your compelling Chain of Evidence in your customer's terms. This defense in our imaginary courtroom might sound like this:

> Ladies and gentlemen of the jury. I stand before you charged with "providing training with no evidence of value to the business." To these charges I plead not guilty!
>
> Clearly, Exhibit A [Figure 10-1] demonstrates that the learners found great value in our program. These two graphs show that for each of our six training sessions, learners clearly felt that they would be able to incorporate the activities into their team efforts and that they would use these skills in their daily activities.
>
> Not only that, but continuing with Exhibit B [Figure 10-2], the learners overwhelmingly said they would recommend this course and that the exercises were relevant to their job.
>
> Ladies and gentlemen of the jury, I submit to you that, at Comcast, written Level 2 knowledge checks are rarely given unless properly validated, therefore Level 2 assessments were conducted via teach-backs, calibration sessions, coaching role-play sessions, and learner self-evaluations. Our chart, Exhibit C [Figure 10-3], clearly demonstrates that the learners believed that the terms and issues were clearly communicated. They were confident in their new knowledge.
>
> But that's only half of the story, esteemed members of the jury. Our private investigators (mystery call vendors) conducted typical

FIGURE 10-1.   Learner Value: Future Application

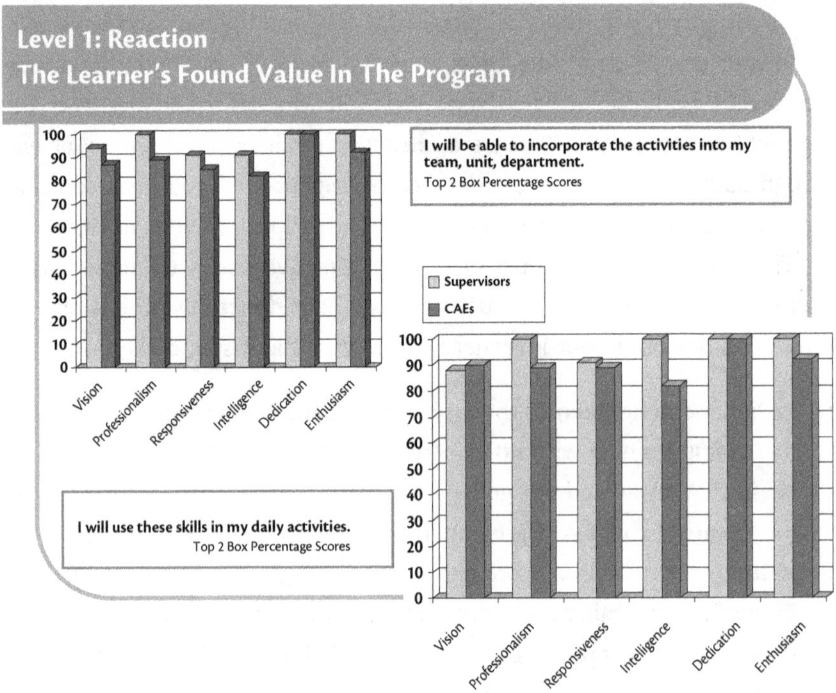

calls to determine the actual skill usage on the job. They proved that the skills of eight out of ten graduates improved, relative to their respective pre-training baselines. Can there be any more compelling evidence? Yes!

Considering that the ultimate judge of on-the-job performance is the customer, jurors will notice that customer satisfaction improved precisely and exactly at the time this training was conducted. All three measurements—the customer feels valued, the representative was knowledgeable, and the representative met his/her commitments—improved from pre-training levels.

Finally, an analysis of the four key performance indicators (digital sales, high-speed Internet sales, service upgrades, and revenue

FIGURE 10-2.   Learner Value: Relevance

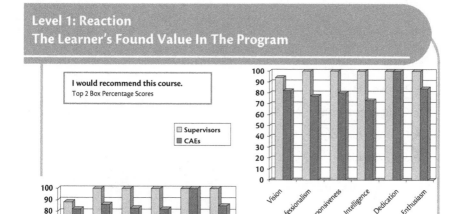

per sale) improved from pre-training levels. Not only that, but the evidence further demonstrates that the sales behavior went from trending downward prior to training to trending upward post-training.

Having been charged with the ultimate training crime (providing training with no evidence of value to the business), the training function at Comcast Cable leveraged the Kirkpatrick Business Partnership Model to create a Chain of Evidence that clearly demonstrates how this initiative provided true value to the business and drove positive results!

FIGURE 10-3.   Learner Value: Knowledge

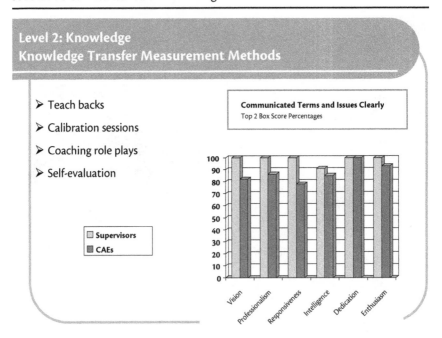

Allen County Department of Transportation

We provide here part of a typical report that would be sent to Allen County's Department of Transportation (A-DOT) executives—the jury—after Jim conducted two impact studies for them. The purpose of such studies would be to demonstrate the value that the county's Human Resources Training and Development Department (HRTDD) was bringing to this government agency and to serve as an evaluation model for the A-DOT in the future. In our fictional example, this program was called "Roller Operations," and the part that is included here shows what the jury wanted to see: a course overview, data, and success factors. Recommendations were also included in the report.

Roller Operations

Course Overview

HRTDD's model for rolling out effective roller operations training through-out A-DOT is to use a "train the trainer" model (TTT). HRTDD trains a certain number of experienced and savvy workers from each of the ten Allen County road districts. They, in turn, conduct eight-hour workshops for employees in the field at their individual work sites. This includes a training video, PowerPoint slide deck, trainer's guide, and participant's guide. As much as is possible, the on-site training includes actual time on the various roller machines. Major components of the training are safety in loading, transporting, and driving the roller equipment, and basic operations of the different kinds of rollers. A-DOT tracks individuals who have received the training. Also, Level 1 and some Level 2 data are collected from TTT participants to ensure a high degree of participant satisfaction and to show that learning has taken place.

Impact Study Methodology

The following steps were taken to obtain data and subjective information on roller operations training in order to accomplish the purposes of this study:

1. Consultant met with HRTDD staff members involved with the roller operations TTT sessions. The purpose was to understand the particulars of the program, view the materials, and assess the current evaluation processes. These meetings also served to determine the best steps for gathering additional information in order to complete this study.

2. To determine specific expectations for each of the four levels, so that the data and information gathered could be evaluated in accordance with HRTDD and stakeholder expectations. The totals for successful contacts are: roller training participants, 10; on-site roller trainers, 6; maintenance supervisors and superintendents, 7; district safety and health managers, 8.

3. A questionnaire was sent to district safety and health managers to determine the nature of any roller incidents that may have occurred since 2002 (see below). The questionnaire explained: "HRTDD is working on how we can improve our training to make a difference on the job. We are focusing on one technical class (roller operations). Some information has been requested that we are unable to gather here. In particular, they want to know how many roller incidents have occurred in your district since 2002. Please provide the following information in order for us to improve the safety and effectiveness of the programs."

Type of incident—that is, rollover or tipover (on its side):

• Date of the incident

• Any employee injury

• The type of equipment damage

• Estimated cost of the incident

4. To collect the information and present it in a report.

Data

Level 1

Nine courses were offered between 4/19/06 and 10/16/07, and evaluated at Level 1. These courses were run specifically for on-site trainers and included 118 participants. The data have been collected and analyzed according to standards set along the way by HRTDD. The analysis is then used to make improvements and spread best practices throughout the department. Specific average scores for each question are (on a five-point scale):

1. Training goals were clearly defined, 4.41
2. Training directly related to my job, 4.45
3. My knowledge increased, 4.40
4. Instructor provided clear and complete answers, 4.46
5. Length of time was just right, 4.23
6. Training materials were easy to use, 4.37

7. Training met my expectations, 4.24
8. Facilities were favorable for learning, 4.34
9. Instructor was knowledgeable, 4.52
10. Hands-on practices were helpful, 4.17
11. Equipment used was favorable for learning, 4.20

Positive comments greatly outweighed negative ones, and care was given to make improvements whenever possible. Following are positive comments recorded via telephone contacts, indicating Level 1 satisfaction:

- I especially liked the hands-on part, because that is how I learn best.

- The trainer was very engaging and knowledgeable about the entire process.

- The on-site trainer was very good. Seemed to care that we learned the safety features.

- It was very helpful that we actually got to try the equipment.

- This was especially good for me, since I had no experience.

Level 2

This level has been addressed by HRTDD in four ways:

1. Formative evaluation methods are woven into the instruction. HRTDD is extremely effective with this technique. For instance, the program developers have imbedded questions in the program so that the instructors can check for understanding. They might also use a method called a teach-back, whereby participants are asked to explain something to the rest of the group.

2. Instructors use checklists to track that correct skills are used during the application portion of the program.

3. "General observation" is used by trainers during the skills sections of the training (e.g., safety procedures and operation of the rollers).

4. Seasoned rollers often have those with less or no experience ride along and observe the loading and unloading procedures, operator safety, and operation techniques on the lot. While there are no specific data available from this, it is an effective teaching technique, as those who know teach those who don't.

Specific data were not collected during the aforementioned methods. Instead, the purpose of these methods was to ensure that there was acquisition of knowledge and skills and to provide the trainers with methods to use in the field. Below are comments recorded via telephone conversations, indicating Level 2 knowledge and skills acquisition:

- I am a new operator and the safety training is what I remember the most. I specifically remember about the loading and unloading, the points of contact, and also not getting too close to the edge.

- I specifically remember about "putting the outer tire down" in case of a predicament.

- While I have been an operator for years, these are always helpful reminders, especially safety.

- I remember about pinch points, getting safely on and off, and how to turn at the end of a patch.

- I learned that the direction you drive the roller is critical to a good patch.

- I appreciated learning about how to stop, the different material I work with, how to park the roller, and about thinness and vibration.

- While the guys won't admit it, they take away something from the training. I hear them talk about it. They are more aware of the dangers.

Level 3

HRTDD staff do employ an effective form of Level 3 evaluation. That is, each trainer is required to make six visits per year to observe trainers conducting actual roller training in the field. Checklists are used to ensure that the trainers are following the prescribed procedures. An additional benefit of these visits is that it increases the rapport among HRTDD, the trainers, and the business sites.

In addition to the on-the-job learning provided by experienced roller operators, there is an element of Level 3 that takes place. Specifically, once the novice operators have spent some time observing the experienced operations, they get a chance to perform the safety and operation aspects of rolling while the seasoned operators watch. This can also include on-the-job observations by trainers and supervisors. Again, while no data are collected, there is a degree of Level 3 feedback and coaching. Several new operators commented that this aspect of on-the-job reinforcement was very helpful.

Here are positive comments recorded via telephone conversations, indicating Level 3 transference of learning to on-the-job behavior:

- As a supervisor, I see people use what they learned—both safety procedures and pinching off at the end of a patch.

- I see my people being more safety conscious with loading and unloading.

- I see the workers talking among themselves when they are rolling. They care about doing it right and being safe. They won't admit it, however.

- In our district, we observe each other and use the buddy system for new rollers. We can see that they are safety conscious and care about the quality of the patch. I think the training helps because they teach us why to use certain techniques.

Level 4

HRTDD staff collected a good bit of Level 4 evidence in the form of data and testimonials. First of all, they had HRTDD and road maintenance supervisors inspect the roads that were reworked. Fortunately, they inspected and took pictures both before and after the work was done. This evidence suggested that the roads were fixed effectively, and that the patching looked sound.

Only time will tell if the seals last for the targeted periods of time, but they will be inspecting and taking additional pictures on a regular basis to see.

Second, they gathered records of safety incidents. These incidents were tracked by district, and compared to past incident reports. The good news is that apparently the learning transferred into safer rolling practices, as the number of critical incidents, and subsequent damage to equipment and injuries to employees, were reduced.

Finally, testimonials from road repair workers and supervisors were collected. They included:

- I learned a lot in training, and was more careful in how I used the equipment, and in how I worked on the roads. I think the work I did was far better than I had done in the past.

- My workers were more conscientious about their work, yet did not take additional time to roll good seals. Many motorists I talked to say they were pleased with the work that was done.

- We were able to stay on time and on budget because fewer mistakes were made.

- I enjoyed the whole training and coaching process. It makes me feel better about my job and the people I work with.

Success Factors

As evident from the preceding data, there is much to say that is positive about the present roller operations training. Below is a list of factors that have contributed to that success.

1. *The model for the training.* The "train the trainer" model is the best way to deploy the amount of training that needs to be done. This sends a consistent learning message to the hundreds of people who end up taking the course, and allows them to learn in the convenience of their workplace. In addition, the combination of video, slide deck, controlled use of equipment, and subsequent on-the-job training seems to be preparing workers well.

2. *The training materials are excellent.* Reviews of the training manuals and comments from participants point to the training materials as the strength of the process. The pictures of various incidents and the video are particularly strong components.

3. *The trainers were seen as strong and conscientious.* Positive comments about the trainers were frequently heard and included descriptions of their being caring, detailed, enthusiastic, and knowledgeable. They were also seen as insightful about the various challenges of training in the field.

4. *Level 1 survey information.* Attention to the Level 1 surveys is seen as a factor that makes the roller operations training successful. Data and soft information have been used to make improvements in the content and delivery of the program.

5. *Level 2 knowledge checks and skills observations.* As mentioned before, attention has been given to building methods into the delivery of the training to ensure that knowledge and skills have been acquired. Together with improvements to Level 1 data, they provide confidence that participants leave the classroom competent to conduct roller operations safely and efficiently. It is this consultant's professional opinion that Level 2 is dealt with effectively.

6. *Conscientious trainers and supervisors.* Telephone interviews with participants made it evident that many of the trainers take their jobs seriously. They want to learn, and especially want to pass along to employees the knowledge that the course offers, plus their own "tricks of the trade." Similarly, several supervisors reported that their jobs were "to reinforce what is learned in training." These factors help to build a strong learning connection between training and the job.

7. *Training is aligned with organizational strategy.* HRTDD takes seriously the mission and values of the agency. Not only do they build their courses and programs with the end in mind (i.e., contributing to the mission and values of the organization), but testimonials from participants support the same, in that many appear to be truly engaged workers.

One final note on the A-DOT case study. It is quite evident that the jury had people on it who appreciated testimonials. They did, however, say that they wanted more data in the future. Since then, the HRTDD team has implemented additional methods to obtain the desired evaluation data.

Some implications of the verdict for training on trial were addressed at the beginning of this chapter. We want to caution you of one more. Many training groups that Jim has worked with have followed all or part of this model, gathered their evidence, and presented their closing arguments to their respective juries. All have been found not guilty of costing more than the value they brought to the business. They have all made good on the challenge of bringing forth true return on expectations. They have crossed the metaphorical bridge between training and business, and now have a nice place to reside (or at least visit) on the other side.

But here's the catch. Business leaders—the members of those juries—now expect them to deliver similar results in the future. But they all agree that's a nice problem to have!

Going Beyond the Data

We would like to mention, and illustrate, an important point. This whole model—our whole industry—is more than numbers, data, and information. It goes beyond our trying to justify our existence. The four levels, our KBPM, are about changing lives and making the world a better place. Many of us have a tremendous opportunity to influence others for the positive.

We would like to introduce two witnesses, one representing the prosecution, and the other who will testify on our behalf as trainers. First is the witness for the prosecution. We do not know his name, but Jim briefly met him at a hotel in southeast Asia. Let's call him "Unknown Window Washer." Note that he is washing windows.

Window Washer—Witness for the Prosecution

Jim was waiting for a taxi outside of a hotel in a southeast Asian city, and he didn't have much better to do than to wander over to a window washer and ask him, "Do you know of any good places to get sushi around here?"

He said, "Not really. Maybe someone inside does."

Jim then asked quite respectfully, "By the way, what is your job here?" Not surprisingly, he responded, "I am a window

washer." Seeing the conversation going nowhere, Jim decided to walk back to the curb and await his cab (but not before snapping his picture).

> ▸ *Testimony:* What the witnesses say when answering questions.

Let's compare the Asia window washer's testimony with that of a fellow window washer, Chai, from a resort in Brunei, whom Jim met the following day. He is our witness for the defense.

Brunei Window Washer—Witness for the Defense

Again, Jim had a little time on his hands, this time in Brunei, and he went over and spoke to Chai. The conversation went something like this:

JIM: Hello. Nice place here. What is your job at this resort?

Chai climbed down from his elevated stand, shook my hand, looked me in the eye.

CHAI: I am part of a team that provides exceptional experiences for our guests. By the way, have you found everything you need here to make your stay enjoyable?

JIM: Wow. Yes I have. And I was not expecting to hear that! So far I have been very impressed with your resort. Tell me, how is it you came to answer my question in the manner that you did?

CHAI: Well, washing windows is only part of my job. I also keep the grounds looking fresh, and the hallways clean. I guess it's just the attitude I have. I do what I can to make for pleasant times for my guests.

JIM: How long have you worked here?

CHAI: About a year.

JIM: What kind of training did you receive?

CHAI: After I was hired, my supervisor sat down with me and told me about the company, and how each of us was an important part in making this the best resort in all of Brunei. He then told me of the training that I would receive, and how it would help me do my job in such a way to make a positive impression on the guests. In training, I not only learned how to cut grass and wash windows, but how to talk with the guests. I am still in training, and always am complimented for doing my job well—both for clean windows and being friendly with people who stay here.

JIM: Nice meeting you, Chai. I am glad you think so highly of yourself and your job.

CHAI: Oh, when you get back to America, would you kindly tell them about how you found Brunei.

JIM: I certainly will, and part of my good feelings about your country have come from talking with you. Thanks so much, Chai.

What a difference between these two people, who were both trained to be window washers! Why is the unknown window washer a witness for the prosecution? It was apparent that, while he may have been trained to wash windows, he did not seem to view his job as anything beyond that. I believe that his windows were clean, but he did little to make me feel welcome at his hotel or in his country. I suppose he just wasn't trained or encouraged to do that.

This represents an indictment on the training he received: believing that once he was beyond Levels 1 and 2, the training manager's job was done. He or she was no longer "on the hook." I feel sorry for that unknown window washer. I suspect he doesn't know what he is missing. (If I went back to that hotel, do you think he would still be working there? Probably not, if a place down the street offered him 50 cents more per hour.)

Chai, by his own admission, was trained and reinforced to be both an excellent window washer and a front-line person when it came to his guests. He believes he is more than a window washer, and his actions showed that he definitely is. He is clearly a witness for the defense (for all trainers) because he demonstrates that comprehensive training, his learning, and subsequent follow-up can help create a concern for service in those people who know that training is not something someone "is sent to." Rather, it is the total learning process by which someone *learns* (Level 2), in order to effectively *perform* a job well (Level 3), in order to bring (personal or career) *benefit* (Level 4), and ultimately to make an *impact* on the organization's bottom line—in this case, the guests of the resort (Level 4). And did you note his parting comment to me? Chai believes he is not just an ambassador for his resort, but also for his country!

Our future lies in helping to develop and encourage the Chais of the world by extending our role as trainers into the workings of the business—and into the lives of the people who have been entrusted to us.

Wendy's Story

When we left off, I had just gotten a call from Jim Kirkpatrick, who had offered to look over a course I had just developed. I am guessing that, if you looked at the cover of this book, you have an idea of what happened next. Jim and I got engaged, and married in 2008. Since we obviously both worked and lived together at that point, I got the immersion course in Kirkpatrick. It became automatic for me to view all training design, development, and implementation through the filter of the Four Levels.

My job continued to be a frustration. I knew the right things to do, yet encountered many roadblocks. I made one final effort to help the others in my company understand the power of the Four Levels. During the time Jim and I were engaged, he was going to be near the corporate office of my company at a time when I was there as well. I convinced him to do a short seminar for my training group at no charge.

The seminar was baffling for both of us. Few people in the room had heard of the Kirkpatrick Model. While Jim's sessions are always lively and interactive, getting anyone to speak this time was difficult and the atmosphere was tense. At the end of the session, everyone filed out of the room. I asked Jim if he had spoken in any venue or capacity where there was not at least one person who hung behind with a question. He said, "Never." I wasn't sure what else I could do to help my team see the value in the Four Levels.

But I couldn't dwell on it too long. I had a wedding to plan!

Key Points

- All of your work up to this point must lead back to your stakeholders'—your jury members'—expectations and expected outcomes.

- You must present your evidence in a four-level sequence in order to create an effective chain of evidence.

- The manner in which you present your case to the jury is just as important as the information you use as support for your arguments. You must be able to tell a "story of value."

- Develop and present a proper blend of data and testimonials.

- Have fun celebrating a positive verdict. Learn from a negative one.

11

Examples from Our Stars

"Never confuse movement with action."
—Ernest Hemingway

WHEN WE CONDUCT SEMINARS, the most frequent request on our Level 1 evaluation forms is "more tools, templates, and examples." So we thought it appropriate to take a chapter of this book to share some exceptional examples of how the KBPM has been used by our stars.

As you review these examples you will see that sometimes the model has been slightly modified or expanded to meet the needs of a given organization. That's okay! The point is that you have a plan and a process, and a reason for them. What's critical for one organization may be different for another.

Highlighting the Importance of Level 3

The Strategic Learning Services department at Edward Jones has developed an impressive modification of the four levels in images, depicted in Figure 11-1.

FIGURE 11-1. Modification of Kirkpatrick Four Levels

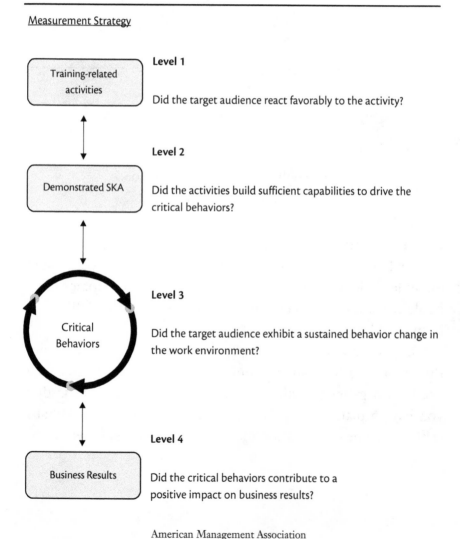

Measurement Strategy

Level 1

Training-related activities

Did the target audience react favorably to the activity?

Level 2

Demonstrated SKA

Did the activities build sufficient capabilities to drive the critical behaviors?

Level 3

Critical Behaviors

Did the target audience exhibit a sustained behavior change in the work environment?

Level 4

Business Results

Did the critical behaviors contribute to a positive impact on business results?

Note that Edward Jones emphasizes Level 3! They realize that there are many factors that can make or break good training, and they focus on those drivers through reinforcement and evaluation.

Edward Jones further defines the variables that can occur at Level 3 and why it is so important to consider each. The circles and arrows in Figure 11-2 show us that these determining drivers can either work for or against the success of an initiative. It is from these circles that the training team determines—with the business stakeholders—which are the most important drivers for a given initiative to encourage the critical behaviors, and whether they are working for or against the application of them.

FIGURE 11-2.   Relationship of Critical Behaviors and Drivers to Business Results

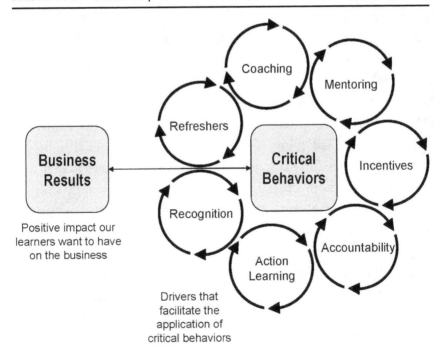

The practical application of this modified model is huge. The arrows offer a supercharged version of the concept. Consider the culture or factors we call drivers as having the potential to either encourage or discourage the application of the critical behaviors by employees who have recently completed a learning event. Further consider the arrows going clockwise as *encouragers* and the arrows going counterclockwise as *discouragers*. Picture, then, working with your stakeholders and other learning professionals to not only identify the key drivers, but also to brainstorm how to get the circles spinning the right way.

Edward Jones has their specific drivers in the diagram. We have placed drivers in the figure that are most applicable to situations that we see in our own work. Here is how we recommend you work with this depiction of the process. Prior to meeting with business stakeholders to determine the required drivers, select what you think will be the most important drivers for the initiative at hand. *Do not* depict which way you think the arrows are going (i.e., revolving clockwise to indicate encouraging and counterclockwise for discouraging). When you meet with your business partners, discuss each driver and elicit their input on (1) whether these indeed are legitimate drivers, and (2) which way the arrows are going. This makes for interesting, enlightening, and at times fiery discussions. But the good news is that the graphic helps them create a feeling of ownership and, thus, a willingness to deal with these important issues and begin to make prudent changes.

Jim was recently working with a company on this and a driver labeled "executive modeling" was discussed. There was much difference of opinion among the business leaders, with the tide eventually turning to admitting that they were *not* good role models of the exact leadership behaviors they were hoping to instill in lower-level leaders. The good news is that they made strides toward getting the arrows moving in the right direction without our having to be confrontational.

> **Business Partnership Tip:** Consider using Figure 11-2 and other simple models to educate business leaders regarding the importance of drivers.

Learning Roles in Company Initiatives

Figure 11-3, developed by Edward Jones' Strategic Learning Services, defines how the scope of an initiative drives the necessary role of the learning professional.

FIGURE 11-3.   Relationship Between Training Focus and Business Focus

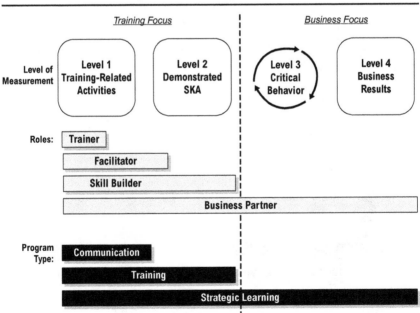

Notice how the roles of trainer, facilitator, and skill builder—all traditional training roles—do not enter the business partnership world. They are showing us how the big chasm exists between Levels 2 and 3. Once you work your way effectively into Levels 3 and 4, you go along way toward creating value for and being able to demonstrate your value to the business.

One final reminder here—they refer to the first two levels as "consumptive metrics" and the Levels 3 and 4 as "impact metrics", as was introduced in Chapter 3. And many business partners (aka jury members) know the difference.

Writing Objectives

Jim has a personal best practice that he learned from working with Booz Allen Hamilton. This is a special tip, just for instructional designers. Instead of using the term "learning objectives" and narrowing the objectives to what is supposed to happen in the classroom or e-learning program (Level 2 stuff), align the objectives with each of the first three levels of the Kirkpatrick Model, as follows:

- Learning Objectives (Level 2)
  - Describe the key elements of the Kirkpatrick Business Partnership Model
  - Identify Don Kirkpatrick's Four Levels of Evaluation
  - Develop a questionnaire for determining stakeholder expectations

- Performance Objectives (Level 3)
  - Conduct a session with key stakeholders to determine success indicators

- o Determine drivers for one of your key initiatives
- o Create a dashboard for a key initiative and send it to stakeholders on a monthly basis

- Business Objectives (Level 4)
  - o Calculate and report the cost savings from a key initiative
  - o Present your case to your corporate jury
  - o Track and report engagement scores and employee retention as related to your new leadership initiative

While you may not be able to reach Level 4 or even Level 3 for every program, create objectives for every level you plan to measure and accomplish. Not only will it help make sure that you align your work with your business partners' expectations, but it will also send a powerful message to your participants: "You are here, not because you have been sent by someone to reward or punish you, but in order for you to learn new knowledge and skills in order for you to perform your job more effectively so you can make a contribution (to yourself, your company, your customers, etc.)." This is the type of training Chai received.

Participant Learning Plan to Initiate Post-Training Reinforcement

This example is from the Region of Waterloo, Ontario, Canada. Rebecca Knapp offers a simple "Learning Plan" template for participants to fill out immediately following their leadership program (Figure 11-4).

FIGURE 11-4   Region of Waterloo Learning Plan Template

Learning Plan

_____

Key area of focus for development in coming year?

_____

_____

Why have you selected this area?

_____

_____

What is your learning goal? (Make it specific, measurable, attainable, realistic, and timely.)

_____

_____

What activities are you planning to achieve your goal?

_____

_____

How will you monitor and measure if your goal is achieved?

_____

_____

Participant Job Aid for
Post-Training Reinforcement

Here is an example of a tool provided to participants in Georgia-Pacific Consumer Products' "Managing Remote Team Members" program (Figure 11-5). Mike Woodard and his team are

FIGURE 11-5. Georgia-Pacific Learning Aid

Module 9: Your Virtual Coaching Journal

This module has two key parts. Part One is designed to be used in this one-day workshop. This section is designed to capture your ideas as responses to management challenges that are posed by the facilitator. The second part is designed to be used as your journal.

Your Coaching Journal has been designed to help you capture your questions and thoughts as you work through the application of what you learned in the one-day workshop. Your coaching responsibilities are fairly simple. Pick a fellow classmate as your virtual coaching partner. Share all your contact information below with your partner. Choose a date every other week for the next 10 weeks when you will connect for 45 minutes to discuss the following:

- What virtual management challenges have you faced since your last conversation and how did you handle them?
- What would you do differently next time, if anything?
- What tools or models from the workshop have you applied and what happened when you tried to apply them?

The Name of Your Coaching Partner: _____

His/her Phone Number: _____

His/her E-Mail Address: _____

The Dates of Your First 5 Coaching Sessions:

1. _____

2. _____

3. _____

4. _____

5. _____

Also, we as a group will be getting together virtually every three weeks to review a model that we discussed in the workshop, share our key learning from being a virtual manager, and pose questions to each other for support and to gain different perspectives on leading virtual team members. Finally, it is expected that each of you will keep your journal current and leverage it as a tool for your management development.

making it as easy as possible for program graduates to do what is expected of them.

The TeamSTEPPS™ Initiative

Here is a comprehensive example of how to plan for and execute an initiative, brought to us courtesy of Heidi King and the United States Department of Defense (DoD) Patient Safety Program team, particularly Sandra Almeida, Mary Salisbury, and Carla Dancy Smith. The DoD developed a systematic approach for implementing and sustaining a patient safety improvement program throughout the military health-care system. The TeamSTEPPS™ (Team Strategies & Tools to Enhance Performance & Patient Safety) team did not start out following the Kirkpatrick Business Partnership Model, since when they planned for this major initiative, the KBPM was not yet in existence. They did, however, use the Kirkpatrick Four Levels as a major foundation. The DoD model and the KBPM share many common principles and processes that are demonstrated below.

Background

The issue of patient safety has been in the forefront of the health-care community's consciousness since the publication of the Institute of Medicine's (IOM) milestone report *To Err Is Human* (Kohn, Corrigan, & Donaldson, 2000). The report brought the epidemic of preventable medical errors to national attention and galvanized clinicians, hospitals, patients, and payors to work together to eliminate these errors and transform the national health-care system to a culture of safety. One of the IOM's key recommendations for reducing patient harm due to medical errors was the establishment of interdisciplinary medical team training programs that are based on proven teamwork training methodologies.

Why team training? Organizations report that ineffective and inadequate communication is the major contributing factor for preventable medical error. Decades of research have shown that team-based collaboration and communication have a positive effect on organizational safety, and that individuals can develop teamwork knowledge, skills, and attitudes through carefully designed team training programs.

TeamSTEPPS™ (Team Strategies & Tools to Enhance Performance & Patient Safety) is a medical team performance improvement program developed by the DoD in response to the call for action. Grounded in the sciences of team performance (Salas & Cannon-Bowers, 2000), organizational change (Kotter, 1996), and training evaluation (Kirkpatrick, 1976), TeamSTEPPS is designed to produce highly effective medical teams that optimize the use of information, people, and resources to deliver the highest quality and safety of patient care. The program includes a comprehensive suite of materials and training curricula to provide healthcare professionals with critical team-related knowledge, skills, and abilities (KSAs) and guide them through implementation and management of a team improvement initiative.

Preliminary program evaluation data and six years of field experience with TeamSTEPPS training has clearly shown that the success of a TeamSTEPPS initiative is contingent on establishment of robust partnerships between TeamSTEPPS Consultants (also called TeamSTEPPS Master Trainers) and the health-care organization—an approach that aligns well with KBPM.

The TeamSTEPP™ Approach

The TeamSTEPPS initiative is executed through a phased approach that has several themes common to the KBPM:

- During each phase there are clear and interrelated roles and responsibilities for the Master Trainers and key stakeholders in the health-care facility who will be implementing the TeamSTEPPS initiative.

- Data and information are collected during each phase and used to guide the facility's forward progress, recognize and overcome barriers during implementation, evaluate program impact, and promote long-term sustained success.

Let's look at these phases and review how they align with the KBPM:

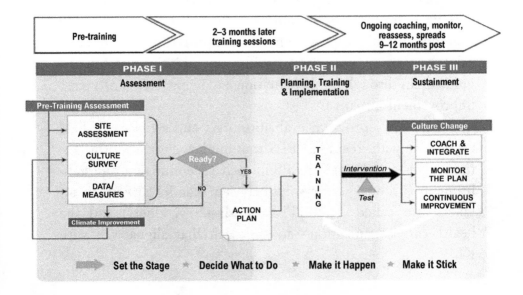

PHASE I: Assessment—Set the Stage

The partnership between the Master Trainers and the health-care organization begins in Phase I, where the goal is to determine organizational readiness for change. Typically, a facility initiates the TeamSTEPPS process by contacting Master Trainers and requesting team training. The reasons for the training requests vary, ranging from "we know we need to change how we care for our patients" to "we just had a bad outcome occur in our hospital and we are seeking advice on how to prevent this from happening again."

It's critical that TeamSTEPPS consultants:

- Understand the vision of the organization

- Listen attentively to the concerns and sense of urgency of the organization

- Engage in transparent discussions regarding the partnership roles and responsibilities throughout the initiative

Based on the organization's responses to a set of focused questions, Master Trainers and the Change Team together determine if the organization is "ready" for a TeamSTEPPS initiative. They are considered ready if they have an identified need for teamwork improvement combined with an organizational climate conducive to change, including key organizational drivers and prerequisites in place.

Master Trainers know that for TeamSTEPPS success and lasting change, organizational leaders must pledge to work together and commit to specified roles and responsibilities along with expectations of accountability. As part of this leadership commitment process, the organization identifies an executive sponsor who will shepherd and regularly monitor the initiative's progress. This local leadership C-suite level leader is kept informed of initiative progress and barriers by an organization-level Change Team, a group of facility key stakeholders who drive the TeamSTEPPS initiative from the frontline. At least one Change Team member is a designated "TeamSTEPPS champion," often a recognized and well-respected clinician and thought leader.

The Change Team identifies a specific opportunity for improvement such as improved communications in the operating room (the jury's expectations) that could be realized with enhanced teamwork. They begin to formulate a vision for "what success would look like" and how they will get there. The Change Team also uses various site assessment tools to determine if the organization has the necessary leadership support, information base, and resources in place to support a successful TeamSTEPPS initiative (organizational prerequisites and drivers). The Master Trainers work closely with the Change Team to assist with observational assessments and alignment of the TeamSTEPPS activities and expected outcomes with existing organizational programs and strategic goals such as patient safety and quality mandates, process improvement methodologies, and patient satisfaction improvement projects. Once the site assessment is complete, the Change Team will have baseline data to guide prioritization of improvement aims and build the chain of evidence to show return on the jury's expectations.

PHASE II: Planning, Training, & Implementation—Decide What to Do and Make it Happen

Phase II is the planning and execution segment of the Team-STEPPS Initiative. It begins with developing the TeamSTEPPS

Action Plan, a written report detailing exactly what an organization intends to do during the Initiative. Using strategies documented in the individualized Action Plan, the group conducts TeamSTEPPS training, and then implements and tests its TeamSTEPPS intervention.

Although creating the Action Plan begins in Phase I, the Change Team actually *commits the Plan to writing* as the essential first activity of Phase II. This Plan functions as the Change Team's "how-to guide" for the entire initiative and solidifies the local executive leadership (C-suite level equivalent decision maker) and team partnership for success. The organization writes its Action Plan by following the "Ten Steps Guide to Developing a TeamSTEPPS Action Plan" (see Figure 11-6).

FIGURE 11-6. Department of Defense TeamSTEPPS™ Report

Ten Steps to Developing a TeamSTEPPS Action Plan

1. Create a Change Team.
2. Define the problem or opportunity for improvement.
3. Define the aim(s) of your TeamSTEPPS intervention.
4. Design a TeamSTEPPS intervention.
5. Develop a plan for testing the effectiveness of your TeamSTEPPS intervention.
6. Develop an implementation plan—for medical team training and for the intervention.
7. Develop a plan for sustained continuous improvement.
8. Develop a communication plan.
9. Putting it all together—write the TeamSTEPPS Action Plan.
10. Review your TeamSTEPPS Action Plan with key personnel.

Step 3, "Define the aim(s) of your TeamSTEPPS intervention," is perhaps the most important step of the Action Plan
since this is where the Change Team states "what success will
look like" in objective, observable, measurable terms that are
meaningful to the organization's stakeholders (jury). This step
is analogous to the KBPM Step 3: Refine expectations to define outcomes.

For example, the organization that stated the expectation of
"improving communications in the operating room" might define the aim as "all surgical teams will use TeamSTEPPS struc-
tured communication techniques and pre-operative briefs for all
cases" (Level 3 outcome) and "reduce post-operative infection
rates by 50%" (Level 4 outcome) within six months of Team-
STEPPS implementation. The stated aims drive the development of all remaining components of the Action Plan. Table 11-
1 gives the similarities (alignment) between the KBPM and the
10-Step model:

Once the Action Plan is completed (or near completion),
TeamSTEPPS Master Trainers and Change Teams collaborate
to deliver TeamSTEPPS training to staff from the work unit(s)
targeted for the TeamSTEPPS intervention. Given this is a
huge effort extending across the world involving 70 hospitals
and over 700 medical and dental clinics, a Train-the-Trainer
methodology is used for scalability.

The final activity of Phase II is implementation of the Team-
STEPPS intervention. This is the point at which staff members
transfer their newly learned teamwork skills to the work environment. The Change Team plays a vital role in this phase, providing ongoing coaching, feedback, and monitoring of expected
team behaviors. As part of the TeamSTEPPS partnership, Master Trainers also communicate (virtually coach) regularly with
the Change Team during this period for multiple purposes, in-

TABLE 11-1. Relationships between KBPM^{SM} and the TeamSTEPPS™ Ten Steps to Developing an Action Plan

KBPM	TeamSTEPPS Ten Steps	Explanation
P: Pledge to work together	Step 1. Assign an executive sponsor and create a Change Team	The Change Team consists of organization leaders and key staff members who will drive the TeamSTEPPS Initiative.
A: Address jury issues	Step 2. Define the problem/opportunity for improvement Step 10. Review Action Plan with key personnel	Problems, opportunities, and expectations are defined by the organization (the jury). Reviewing the action plan with key organizational personnel ensures the plan has captured the jury's expectations.
R: Refine expectations to define outcomes	Step 3. Define aims	Aims are written in objective, observable, measurable outcomes, many of which the health-care organization already tracks and reports to leadership such as adverse patient events and measures of the quality of care. Aims are derived from the more generic expectations stated during "problem definition" (Step 2).
T: Target critical behaviors and required drivers	Step 6. Develop an implementation plan for the TS intervention Step 7. Develop a plan for sustained continuous improvement	The plans for TeamSTEPPS intervention implementation and for sustained continuous improvement both address key organizational drivers that facilitate transfer of critical behaviors to the job, such as coaching and feedback, periodic assessments of team behaviors, reinforcements, integration of team principles into everyday operations, and ongoing impact measurements.

(continues)

TABLE 11-1.   (Continued)

KBPM	TeamSTEPPS Ten Steps	Explanation
N: Necessities for success	Step 8. Develop a communication plan Step 10. Review Action Plan with key personnel	Master Trainers must understand the organizational factors and drivers at the onset. The goal of the communication plan is to generate initial and long-term TeamSTEPPS initiative support from key organizational stakeholders (e.g., executive and frontline leaders, staff, patients) to promote successful implementation, sustainment, and spread of positive changes. When key personnel review the action plan they are specifically asked to identify potential barriers to initiative success and offer solutions.
E: Execute the initiative	Step 4. Design a TeamSTEPPS intervention Step 6. Design an implementation plan	During Steps 4 and 6, Change Teams in collaboration with Master Trainers identify the TeamSTEPPS tools and strategies (the intervention) that will best achieve the organization's stated aims, design a TeamSTEPPS training program based on the aims and desired intervention, and then create a plan for implementing the intervention. These plans will be executed during the second part of Phase II.
R: Return on Expectations	Step 10. Review Action Plan with key personnel	Presenting the final Action Plan to key organizational stakeholders ensures that the initiative is structured to result in their expected outcomes.

cluding tracking of initiative progress, collecting evaluation data and information, and providing subject matter expertise and ongoing cheerleading support.

Prior to wide implementation of TeamSTEPPS, Change Teams are encouraged to test the intervention with a small number of staff, or one department/work unit. The purpose of this activity is to refine intervention processes, identify barriers and solutions, and determine (through small-scale measurements) if the intervention is likely to lead to achievement of the stated aims.

PHASE III: Sustainment—Make It Stick

The goal of Phase III is to sustain and spread improvements in teamwork performance, clinical processes, and outcomes resulting from the TeamSTEPPS initiative. During this phase, users integrate teamwork skills and tools into daily practice, monitor and measure the ongoing effectiveness of the TeamSTEPPS intervention, and develop an approach for continuous improvement and spread of the initiative throughout the organization or work unit. These teamwork activities result in improvements at all levels—individual, team, and organizational—accelerating advancements toward the patient safety goals and their specific stated aim(s).

This is the phase during which the health-care organization takes on increasing responsibility and ownership for their initiative, integrating TeamSTEPPS behaviors and principles into "normal business processes." TeamSTEPPS Master Trainers gradually reduce their involvement until they provide only ad hoc subject-matter expertise. Sustainment is managed by the local Change Team through facilitation of organizational drivers, such as real-time coaching, active observation of team performance, and feedback to staff members in the workplace. Other essential sustainment activities for the organization include continuing staff training of teamwork skills (newly launched Trainers further train the local staff) through refresher courses and newcomer orientation, implementation of systems to reward teamwork behaviors and hold staff accountable, and ongoing effectiveness measurements. In summary, these activities focus on execution and monitoring of the required drivers.

So What? The TeamSTEPPS™ Evaluation Methodology

Evaluation is an inherent part of the TeamSTEPPS program. From the beginning, the TeamSTEPPS design team understood that multilevel evaluations are essential for successful planning, implementation, and sustainment of organizational change. Table 11-2 outlines elements of the TeamSTEPPS evaluation methodology that align with the KBPM. At the core of the TeamSTEPPS evaluation model are Kirkpatrick's Four Levels of training evaluation (Kirkpatrick, 1976). Our evaluation model also includes measurements of organizational necessities (prerequisites), required drivers, and individual pre-training motivation and readiness to learn—assessments that were added based on our lessons learned and the sciences of team training (Salas and Cannon-Bowers, 2001, 2000) and organizational change (Kotter, 1996; Kotter & Rathgeber, 2005).

In addition to answering the core question of whether Team-STEPPS training produced the organization's expected results, evaluation provides several other meaningful benefits:

- Buy-in from key facility leaders and frontline staff

- Staff enthusiasm

TABLE 11-2. TeamSTEPPS™ Evaluation Methodology

Level of Evaluation	What Is Measured	When Measured and Why
Level 4 Results	The degree to which team behavior change on the job produced the organization's intended results—e.g., improved patient outcomes, clinical processes, staff and patient satisfaction; staff retention; reduced malpractice claims and costs; reduced adverse patient events	• Prior to training, if possible and applicable, to provide baseline data • At periodic intervals after training to show continual improvements in intended results during progressive TeamSTEPPS skills implementation and practice
Required Drivers	Characteristics of the organizational work environment that facilitate transfer and long-term integration of learned KSAs to the job—e.g., organizational learning climate; visible leadership (executive, supervisory, frontline) support; an initiative plan; on-going training including coaching, reinforcement, refresher, new staff; resource availability; on-going measurement; opportunities to practice	• Prior to training, if possible, to identify potential barriers (and develop strategies to overcome) to training transfer to the job • At periodic intervals after training to identify barriers and facilitators to TeamSTEPPS initiative progress (especially Level 3 changes)
Level 3 Critical Behaviors	The degree to which participants change their behavior on the job based on what they learned. Did they use the intended TeamSTEPPS tools and strategies?	• Prior to training, if possible, to provide a baseline of team performance and to identify opportunities for team improvements • At periodic intervals after training to: —assess improvements in team performance —monitor initiative and learning progress —coach, reinforce, and improve team skills

TABLE 11-2. (Continued)

Level of Evaluation	What Is Measured	When Measured and Why
Level 2 Learning	The degree to which participants acquired the intended TeamSTEPPS knowledge, skills, and attitudes	• Sometimes prior to training, if applicable and feasible, to establish pre-training baseline • Usually during and immediately following the training event • Future learning measures will likely include assessments at periodic intervals after the training event to demonstrate on-going learning
Level 1 Reaction	The degree to which participants reacted favorably to the training—including enjoyment, perception of training relevance to their jobs, confidence in ability to use it in the work environment	• Immediately following the training event to assess immediate reactions to training
Individual Pre-training Experiences and Attitudes	Participant pre-training experiences and attitudes about the value of teamwork, measured prior to the training event, that may impact their readiness and motivation to learn	• Immediately prior to training to help explain L1 and L2 results • Can also be measured during facility site assessments (Phase I) to help determine a unit's readiness for training and to inform training preparation strategies

- Monitoring of initiative progress and required drivers
- Identification of opportunities for continued training program improvement
- Validation of the TeamSTEPPS program value through creation of a "Chain of Evidence"

However, perhaps the greatest value of the TeamSTEPPS evaluation methodology is not directly related to its assessment benefits. The information collected at various evaluation levels also provides valuable guidance to the business partnership (Master Trainers and facility Change Team members) throughout the three TeamSTEPPS phases regarding best "next steps" to ensure continued forward progress toward successful achievement of the intended results.

References

Kirkpatrick, D. L. (1976). "Evaluation of Training." In R. L. Craig, ed., *Training and Development Handbook.* New York: McGraw-Hill, Chap. 18, pp. 1–27.

Kohn, L. T., J. M. Corrigan, & M. S. Donaldson. (eds.). (2000). *To Err Is Human: Building a Safer Health System.* Washington, DC: Committee on Quality of Health Care in America, Institute of Medicine, National Academy Press.

Kotter, J. P. (1996). *Leading Change.* Boston: Harvard Business School Press.

Kotter, J., and H. Rathgeber. (2005). *Our Iceberg Is Melting: Changing and Succeeding under Any Conditions.* New York: St. Martin's.

Salas, E., S. Almeida, H. King, E. H. Lazzara, K. A. Wilson, M. Salisbury, et al. (in press). "What Are the Critical Success Factors for Implementing Team Training in Health Care?" *Joint Commission Journal on Quality and Patient Safety.*

Salas, E., & J. Cannon-Bowers. (2001). "The Science of Training: A Decade of Progress." *Annual Review of Psychology* 52: 471–99.

Salas, E., & J. A. Cannon-Bowers. (2000). "The Anatomy of Team Training." In S. Tobias & J. D. Fletcher, eds., *Training and Retraining: A Handbook for Business, Industry, Government, and the Military.* New York: Macmillan, pp. 312–35.

TeamSTEPPS™ Instructor Guide. [TeamSTEPPS™: Team Strategies & Tools to Enhance Performance and Patient Safety; developed by the Department of Defense and published by the Agency for Healthcare Research and Quality.] AHRQ Publication No. 06-0020. Rockville, MD: Agency for Healthcare Research and Quality; September 2006.

White House Forum on Health Reform. (2009). March 5. *Proceedings.* Washington, DC: Government Printing Office.

12

Call to Action

"Be the change you wish to see in the world."
—Mahatma Gandhi

WE SINCERELY HOPE this book stirs your heart and your mind to action. Just as our superstars called forth in this book, you will be, in Wendy's word, a trailblazer, part of helping to re-shape and revitalize the learning industry. We truly believe that it is imperative you make the transition from checkmark training to true strategic business partner. The day of reckoning has ar-rived. You have received your wakeup call.

This book is also a reminder of our effort to bring forth answers to the questions many professionals have, and especially for their requests for a message of hope. Indeed, the hope is that there has never been a better opportunity for us—consultants, training managers, instructional designers, human resource gen-eralists, OD professionals, training software developers—to have a positive impact on our industry, our businesses, and our economy. There is nothing we would like better than for you to apply this model and get closer to the business, and then become an ambassador for the rest of the learning and business community. We hope you will take the initiative in whatever situation you find yourself and use a disciplined, logical, and passionate way of creating and demonstrating your value to the business.

We were sitting at the breakfast table a couple of days ago and Wendy asked, "Jim, what if this doesn't work for some people?" Jim felt like saying, "No way that could happen," but didn't. It could. There are a number of ways you could be frustrated while trying to cross the great bridge. Failure would most likely occur as a result of (1) skipping important elements of the process, (2) not scoping your initiative in line with expectations and success indicators, or (3) somebody else stonewalling you.

You have a lot to say about either of the first two possible derailers. The third may be more out of your control. What do we suggest? Take a tip from Melanie Barnes of the Allen County DOT. Her team spent a lot of time assessing which districts in Allen County would most likely bring about a successful pilot. As I listened to them discuss this question, they seemed to focus on where they would get the strongest business/management support. In other words, where they would find business partners who "get it" and will be actively supportive of the process.

That is our advice to you who are being stonewalled or who anticipate you will be. Find one or more enlightened business partners—sponsors, champions, executives, senior managers, whatever you want to call them—and approach them about this new undertaking that will create great leverage for their business results. Work with them; create success, showcase it, and then go before the jury of *their* peers to show them the power of what you did as collaborating professionals. And if possible, get your champion to be one of your star witnesses. In legal parlance, these people are called *commissioners in chancery*.

> ▸ *Commissioner in chancery:* A business partnership–oriented professional who can either conduct impact studies for your organization or guide you as you do them.

What if everything you try doesn't work? No one is interested in the same vision you have for accountability, discipline, contribution, partnering, and results? Talk with us or other professionals acquainted with these challenges. There are ways to crack even the toughest eggs.

Asking for Help and Building a Community

The old adage is true: A prophet is seldom respected in his/her own country. There are two specific ways that an outside consultant who specializes in the KBPM can really make a difference in your organization. First, that individual can help you shape and present a case for business partnership. Second, he or she can help you conduct and present an impact study.

We strongly encourage you to take action with what you have read. One significant way you can do that is to select a high impact, mission-critical program or other initiative and decide to run it by using this model. We invite you to e-mail us and tell us about it. It doesn't have to be in any specific format as long as you provide us with enough details to form an impression. Following our review of it, we will:

1. Provide feedback and recommendations as to how to proceed.
2. Add you to our Kirkpatrick Business Partnership community, where you will receive updates, best practices, and tools.
3. If needed, put you in contact with other like-minded trainers who can support your work.

Being a trailblazer isn't easy. But if no one blazed a new trail, we would still be living in caves and heating our foraged food over a fire, right? We hope that you will join us in forging a new, enhanced role for learning professionals. If we all work together, we can make this a reality.

Note: It is not surprising that Wendy asked me what we would do if the business partnership model or this book "didn't work." Here is the conclusion of her story.

Wendy's Story

After Jim and I got married in August 2008, I had a big decision to make. I think most of my co-workers thought I was just going to quit my job. But I'm not a quitter! Jim and I considered many ideas, including my starting a company. In the end, we decided that, with the impending recession, it would make sense for me to stay in my current job and stick it out for a while longer. To get my mind off my internal conflicts, I would continue my education, and of course I would accompany Jim to many seminars and events. So, it was decided.

As you know, the best-laid plans often go astray. In December 2008 there was a corporate downsizing and I got laid off. Looking back over my career and keeping things in perspective, I quickly saw that this was another one of those lucky events for me. I wasn't happy at that company, and I was being given my own "personal summons" to find a job that was more in line with my values and beliefs. I was proud of my accomplishments at that job: I established a training advisory committee, designed a comprehensive sales and customer service training program, created a valuable job aid used throughout the company, and established a train-the-trainer tool that saved thousands of hours of prep time for sales meetings. I could definitely move forward knowing that I had done all I could to promote learning and business partnership in that company!

For those of you who dream of starting your own training or consulting company, take it from me that keeping your job in corporate America is far, far easier! I spent the months following my layoff soaking up as much information as I could about the many facets of small business ownership. I had many a sleepless night thinking about legal issues, financing, marketing, and everything else that a corporation takes care of for you so you have the time to focus on the real issue: the content.

Which brings us to today. I have told this story because I feel it is a realistic account of what it's like to be one of the trailblazers, like our star witnesses. This book shows you their accomplishments, but it doesn't always highlight the hard work and challenges behind them. So I humbly offer my story as a realistic counterpoint. With that said, I want you to be encouraged and empowered by my tale! In the course of fewer than seven years I not only learned a lot about training but also became a change agent and advocate for training value and business partnership. A lot of progress was made in a relatively short period of time within a traditional, slow-changing company. My accomplishments there were things that I was told "could not be done." And they happened in a period of about five years. Just imagine what *you* can do if you have more experience or tenure, or work for a company that embraces change and progress!

I look back on my experience with that company as the many steps on a journey toward a better business world. While I did not singlehandedly change the culture of the company I worked for, I brought them awareness that there is another way to conduct training and to work together. I believe I was a key player in a positive change pattern. I think they will make continual progress toward creating training with substance and a culture of business partnership.

In the meantime, I feel lucky to be able to communicate such a valuable and *hopeful* message to other learning professionals by way of this book. I know that I have found my calling. I strive to help others find theirs. There is so much that training can do to help companies and individuals find success. I can't wait to get out of bed every morning to share the message!

Index